JASON LAKHDARI

HOW TO BUILD A WEBSITE WITH HTML5 AND CSS3

SITERAW

HOW TO BUILD A WEBSITE
WITH
HTML5 AND CSS 3

HOW TO BUILD A WEBSITE WITH HTML5 AND CSS3

BUILDING YOUR WEBSITE HAS NEVER BEEN SO EASY

JASON LAKHDARI

WWW.SITERAW.COM

ISBN: 1984030205
ISBN-13: 978-1984030207

W W W . S I T E R A W . C O M

CONTENTS

HOW TO BUILD A WEBSITE WITH HTML5 AND CSS3

BUILDING YOUR WEBSITE HAS NEVER BEEN SO EASY

JASON LAKHDARI

PREFACE

PREFACE

FOREWORD

Maybe you believe that you aren't ready to learn how to build a website from scratch, that it's too advanced, too difficult, too complicated, etc... but don't worry, the HTML and CSS languages that we will discover throughout this book are incredibly easy to understand and to use. It's not uncommon to see kids as young as ten years old learn web development and start creating their own websites. Using HTML and CSS is no more difficult than learning grammar or conjugation, in fact it's often much easier. All you need to know is how to turn on a computer, the rest is explained in depths in this book.

WHAT YOU WILL LEARN

In order to build a functional website we will need to know two computing languages, HTML and CSS, which we will discover progressively in this book.

The course itself is divided into five parts.

1. HTML5 Basics: a quick introduction to the world of web development, followed by the basics of the HTML language. What tools do you need to build a website? How can we see real time results? How can we add text, images and create links?

2. CSS3 Design: we will then introduce the CSS language which is complementary to HTML. CSS allows us to modify the design of our site: add color, background, borders, change the size or fonts of the text, and even play with slightly more advanced features such as gradients or transparency.

3. Website Creation: this is where things get serious as we'll learn how to build a fully functional website, using many of the principles we covered in the first two parts. You'll be surprised when you realize how easy building a website can be.

4. Advanced Features: moving further into the realm of web development, we will learn about all the advanced features of HTML and CSS such as tables, forms, audio and video handling, and even the quite novel concept of responsive design.

5. Conclusion: this last part is mainly about what's left to learn, including how to send your website on the Internet and thus make it accessible to the entire world at all time. We'll also introduce a few additional web technologies such as Javascript, PHP, ASP.NET and AJAX.

And at the very end of this book you'll find two mementos: the lists of HTML tags and CSS properties, respectively.

HOW TO READ THIS BOOK

FOLLOW THE CHAPTER ORDER

The best way to read this book is... like a book, meaning chapter by chapter.

Unlike many technical courses where it's common to read diagonally and skip some chapters, for this course I recommend you follow the order in which it's written unless you are already somewhat experienced with web development as well as the HTML and CSS languages.

PRACTICE WHAT YOU LEARN

The key to learning and remembering what you will read in this book is to practice regularly, ideally at the same time you're going through the course.

Don't wait until you've finished the entire book to turn on your computer and start coding.

VISIT SITERAW.COM

Make sure to visit SiteRaw (*http://www.siteraw.com*) if you ever have questions concerning a particular aspect of this course.

In addition, you will also find live demonstrations of the examples showed in this book.

INTRODUCTION

You would like to create your own website but you think it's too complicated? Don't look any further, this is the tutorial you need. There is nothing difficult or complicated in creating websites, and thanks to this tutorial you will learn very quickly how to build a website from scratch.

This course is designed for beginners who know nothing about web development and are only waiting for one thing: a complete lesson, from A to Z, with simple explanations and concrete examples.

In this tutorial, you will learn how to:

- Add text to your website
- Insert images, videos and graphic effects
- Create links between your pages
- Build a navigation menu

- Change the background, color, size or font
- Position elements as you want
- And much more

Ready to build your website? All you need to do is read the following chapters, no prerequisites.

PART I

HTML5 BASICS

HOW ARE WEBSITES CREATED?

Welcome to this course on how to create a website from A to Z. This is the first chapter and, as such, it will serve mostly as an introduction to the world of web development. You probably have quite a few questions, so let's start with the most obvious one: how do websites work?

Let's find out...

HOW WEBSITES WORK

Before we start building websites from scratch, it is best to have a least a general understanding of how the web functions.

You will learn everything you need to know in this chapter.

How are websites created?

That's a good question. Almost everyone uses the web these days, so this explanation may seem redundant, but it's important to talk about it before diving into the more concrete aspects of website creation. To browse the web, you need a certain program unironically called a web browser.

You may recognize one of these icons:

A few major web browsers

These are the main browsers you use to navigate the web. Web browsers are in fact very simple programs.

All they contain is a few buttons, an address bar, a TDI system (tabs) and... an HTML rendering engine, also known as the browser's graphical layout engine.

Without a layout engine, a web browser is pretty much useless. The layout engine is what:

- Reads the code present on a web page
- Interprets and translates it
- Renders it into what most people commonly associate with a website (header, menu bar, text, links and so on)

And all this happens every time you load a different page! Pretty fast...

To summarize, before a web page can be displayed in a way that is readable to the user, it must first be fetched and interpreted by the web browser.

HTML AND CSS

You keep talking about HTML and CSS, what are they?

HTML and CSS are two computer languages used to create websites.

You remember when I said that the browser fetches "code" from a web page and renders it? This is the code I'm talking about, HTML and CSS.

The HTML and CSS languages are the basis of how nearly all modern websites work, including SiteRaw. They are simply essential and used pretty much everywhere.

HTML and CSS for building websites

What you need to remember is that HTML and CSS are the languages "spoken" by web browsers. To get a web browser to display what you want on your website (be it a text block, a video, a series of images), you need to speak to it in its native languages: HTML and CSS.

 But why learn two languages? Won't that make things more complicated? Isn't one language good enough?

You're probably thinking that having to learn two languages will make the whole process twice as long, twice as complicated and twice as hard... not even close.

If anything, having two languages for web development makes things less complicated, not more. You will understand why at the end of this chapter. For now just imagine that HTML is like the alphabet and CSS is like the numeral system. This analogy makes no sense, but it illustrates how having two languages can makes things easier.

HTML and CSS are both complimentary and fill completely different roles.

THE ROLES OF HTML AND CSS

As we already stated, to communicate with the web browser you need to speak a language he understands. Luckily for you, he speaks at least two languages which you can learn easily: HTML and CSS.

 Modern web browsers can also interpret other languages, such as Javascript. And if you add browser plugins, the list grows even more. For this tutorial, we will stick to HTML and CSS as they are the foundations of almost any website.

But why two languages? As I mentioned, they both fill two different and very specific roles.

- HTML (HyperText Markup Language) is a **markup language**. Its role is to store information and send information to the web browser. It mainly describes the structure and semantics of a web page. This language appeared in 1991, at the very beginning of the world wide web.
- CSS (Cascading Style Sheets) is a **style sheet language**. Its role is to manage the look of a web page, layout, positioning, color and so forth. CSS was introduced to complement HTML in 1996.

If you want a tangible example of the uses of both HTML and CSS, consider this.

- **HTML says**: This is the title of my page, this is my menu and this is my main text.
- **CSS says**: I want my title in bold and red, my menu floating on the right and my main text to be slightly smaller but underlined.

If you remember that HTML is used to write content, and CSS to stylize that content, then believe me you have already learned 95% of what is to know.

You could technically create a website only using HTML, but

the results wouldn't be very aesthetically pleasing.

CSS, however, requires HTML code to work. For this reason we will start by learning the basics of HTML development before moving on to CSS in the second part of this tutorial.

HTML and CSS working together

We will start building websites in HTML only, and they will be quite ugly... but be patient, once we get to part II of this course, we'll introduce CSS and you'll see your pages magically become beautiful.

THE DIFFERENT VERSIONS OF HTML AND CSS

There have been several versions of HTML and CSS since their creation, and each update brought significant changes to the way websites are developed. In the first version of HTML, you couldn't even display images!

Here is a brief history of both languages.

THE HISTORY OF HTML

- **HTML 1.0**: This was the very first release of HTML, in 1991. A limited language, made for very few web developers and having even less features, there wasn't much you could do with HTML 1.0 bar getting some text on the web.
- **HTML 2.0**: The second version of HTML appeared in 1994. Barely an upgrade from HTML 1.0, this version simply added a few more features on top of it.
- **HTML 3.0**: We have to wait until 1996 to see the first serious update. It's only with HTML 3.0 that many of the components we commonly associate with current websites became available for web development usage. HTML 3.0 added many possibilities to the language such as the inclusion of tables, scripts, floating text around images and more.
- **HTML 4.0**: Appearing for the first time in 1998, HTML marked a significant evolution of HTML standards and proposed features such as the use of frames, more complex tables and refined forms. But the major improvement over its predecessors was the inclusion of style sheets, the famous CSS.
- **HTML 5.0**: This is the current version of the HTML language, and the one we will be studying in this course. It appeared in 2014, although it was available much

earlier for testing. As for its features... keep reading this tutorial, you'll discover them soon enough.

You may also have heard of a sixth version, xHTML. Officially, it's a completely different language from HTML, but there are much more similarities than distinctions. xHTML (eXtensible HyperText Markup Language) appeared in 2000, between HTML 4.0 and HTML 5.0, with the goal of providing more structure and better standards for web development. While many of its features remain in HTML 5.0, this language is no longer used as we have returned to "basic" HTML.

THE HISTORY OF CSS

• **CSS 1.0**: Founded in 1996, the goal of this language was (and still is) to dissociate document content from document presentation. Before that, the only way to properly design your website was through pure HTML, which was never the purpose of that language. And the "solutions" that web developers devised to circumvent HTML's limitations were... special. Those who suffered the trauma of pre-CSS web design don't often talk about it.

• **CSS 2.0**: This version appeared in 1999 and brought a few improvements, namely in the way elements were positioned on a web page. It was also a way to satisfy those who were still skeptical of CSS and refused to use it or bother learning about it.

• **CSS 3.0**: The current version of CSS and the one we will be studying in this tutorial. CSS 3.0 brought a TON of new features to web developers such as gradients, rounded edges, shadows and even interactive elements!

TEXT EDITORS

Now that you understand how websites work and the purpose of HTML and CSS, you're probably wondering how websites are created. Specifically, what type of software do you need to build web pages.

There are quite a few.

In fact, the list of every program you could use to build a website is far too consequential to list here, so we'll start with the simplest and least obvious one: Notepad.

Yes, seriously

Notepad or any text editor is more than enough to build a website from scratch.

But while Notepad is sufficient to create a website, there are more appropriate text editors that are designed distinctly for that purpose.

I will present three text editors intended specifically for web development.

They are in my opinion the best tools for creating websites.

- **Brackets**: A free, modern, open-source text editor available for Windows, Mac or Linux. It offers many features while retaining an ergonomic and accessible interface. This is the software I recommend for web development.
- **Sublime Text**: One word, simplicity. This text editor has the main advantage of being easy to use, uncluttered and convenient from the start.
- **Microsoft Visual Studio**: The heavyweight of programming and website creation. Much more than a simple text editor, Visual Studio is an integrated development environment (IDE) that supports many programming languages in addition to allowing you to code in HTML and CSS. This is by far the most complete tool for building websites. I don't recommend it for beginners as it is rather large and many of its components

are unnecessary for basic web development, but if you already have Visual Studio feel free to use it.

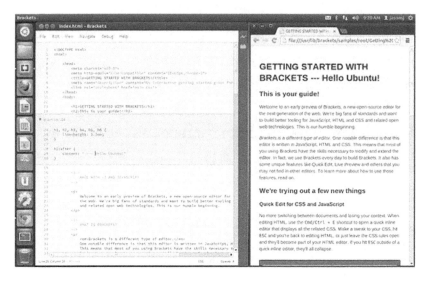

Brackets, the text editor I recommend

Whichever text editor you decide to use, the basic principles of building websites remain identical. The choice is mainly for cosmetics and personal preference.

You may also have heard of WYSIWYG (What You See Is What You Get) programs such as Adobe Dreamweaver or even Microsoft Word. These are very easy to use even without knowing HTML and CSS, but since the HTML and CSS code is auto-generated and is not always of the best quality, sooner or later you'll have to edit it by hand. They are good software but I don't propose them for this tutorial.

Now that we have our text editor we can talk about the last essential element... the web browser.

WEB BROWSERS

Do you know what a web browser is?

I briefly mentioned them at the beginning of this chapter, but since we're starting from scratch (the purpose of this website after all) I'll recapitulate the basics.

- A web browser is a program that allows you to navigate the web.
- To render web pages a browser needs a layout engine.
- The job of the layout engine is to convert HTML and CSS code to a readable format.

This is where things get slightly complicated.

Not every web browser uses the same layout engine.

For example, here is a list of the major layout engines and their respective browsers. You may recognize a few.

- **Trident**: Internet Explorer
- **WebKit**: Safari, Chrome (old), Chromium (old)
- **Gecko**: Firefox, SeaMonkey
- **Blink** (based on WebKit): Chrome, Chromium
- **EdgeHTML**: Microsoft Edge

What this means is, in theory, not all browsers will render your website the exact same way.

Luckily, as of today, most web browsers are fully up to standards and the differences in layout are minimal to non-existent.

Not all browser use the same layout engine

But that wasn't always the case.

To complicate matters further, there are multiple different versions of the same browser: Firefox 3, Firefox 4, Internet

Explorer 8, Internet Explorer 9 and Internet Explorer 10.

And that's not even counting the sub-versions of each browser, or the browsers for mobile phone, tablet and other electronic devices. If modern browsers all display your website in a nearly identical fashion, that's not always the case with older browsers or older versions thereof.

That is why many web developers recommend having several browsers installed to test your website. It's not necessarily something I advocate, as the number of users of outdated browsers is constantly shrinking thanks to the auto-update component, but it's something to consider. If you're really paranoid and still want to install several web browsers, pick ones with different rendering engines. Example: Safari for WebKit, Microsoft Edge for EdgeHTML and Firefox for Gecko.

SMARTPHONE WEB BROWSERS

In addition to the browsers described above, be aware that there are also web browsers for mobile phones, especially smartphones.

More and more people navigate the web from their smartphone, so you must at least know the basics of mobile browsers. Don't panic, they are usually just lighter versions of desktop browsers.

- **Apple iPhone**: The iPhone uses Safari Mobile, a lighter but nonetheless very complete version of Safari.
- **Windows Phone**: Windows Phone mobiles include either Internet Explorer Mobile or Edge Mobile.
- **Android**: Android uses... Chrome Mobile. Once again, a lighter version of the desktop browser.
- **Blackberry**: People still use these? Blackberries are the exception to the rule as they have their own browser, but it's based on WebKit just like Chrome and Safari.

While they are much lighter and less refined, smartphone browsers support most of the latest HTML and CSS features. In addition, the auto-update system guarantees that the users will have the latest version available.

This concludes this introductory chapter (finally). Let's start building websites.

START BUILDING YOUR WEBSITE

Alright. You've installed the software you need? You should now have a text editor to create your website and at least one web browser to test it. In this chapter, we are going to start the actual coding of your website. We will cover the basics of the HTML language and create our first web page.

Let's go!

YOUR FIRST HTML PAGE

As I said, you should now have a text editor installed. It doesn't matter if you use Brackets, Visual Studio, Sublime Text or even Notepad. For this tutorial we will use Brackets but process will be similar whichever text editor you use.

Now open it.

Some editors will automatically create a new document for you. With brackets, you will have a "demo" HTML page already filled with HTML code.

A demo HTML page under Brackets

Erase everything so you have a blank page.

 So how do we write HTML code?

If you don't see the demo HTML page, just create a new document under File > New.

That's up to you. I suggest you type *"Welcome to my first HTML page!"* or whatever else you want to write.

Your first HTML page

All that's left to do is to save our web page and load it in the browser. To save an HTML document, go to File > Save as you would do with any program.

Save the file where you want, for example on your Desktop or in a folder, and give it the name you want. The only requirement is that it must end with .html. By default under Brackets it will be named index.html.

Now go to your Desktop or the folder in which you saved

your file and simply double-click on it. It will show up in your browser (you should see *"Welcome to my first HTML page!"* or whatever text you decided to type).

Hitherto, nothing too complicated.

Yes, but wait... if that was all there was, it wouldn't be any fun. In addition to simply typing text as we've done, we also need to send instructions to the browser about what exactly is going on in our web page. For example, we need a way to tell the browser: "this is text", "this is an image", "this is a link"...

The way we do that is by using HTML tags.

HTML TAGS AND ATTRIBUTES

As we mentioned, HTML code isn't used only to display text. You need to be able to send data to the browser.

To do this in HTML, you use tags.

HTML TAGS

On an HTML page, in addition to text, you'll find another element: HTML tags.

These tags are not seen on the screen by the end user but are necessary to communicate information about the page to the web browser.

HTML tags are easily recognizable: they start with < and end with > (angle/pointy brackets).

For example: `<siteraw>`.

 There is no `<siteraw>` tag in HTML (yet?). It's a fictitious example. We'll find out about real HTML tags in just a moment.

Tags serve many functions, from indicating the type of text they surround to layering your web page... they can even ask the browser to fetch another document: a Javascript script, a CSS style sheet, a video... or even another HTML page altogether.

We distinguish two types of tags in HTML: **paired tags** and **standalone tags**.

PAIRED TAGS

Also called double tags, these are the most common. They are opened, very often contain some text in the middle, and are closed by writing the same tag with a slash "/".

Example:

```
<siteraw>SiteRaw</siteraw>
```

The first `<siteraw>` indicates the opening of the tag, and it is closed further on with `</siteraw>`. Everything between the two is considered belonging to the fictitious "siteraw" tag.

Similarly, anything not between the tags doesn't belong to it.

```
Welcome to <siteraw>SiteRaw</siteraw>, enjoy
your stay.
```

These tags go by pairs, hence the name paired tags.

STANDALONE TAGS

Standalone tags, often called single tags, orphan tags or self-closing tags, are generally used to insert an element (image, video, line break) into a web page.

There is no need to delineate the start and end of an image, to take the most common example of their use. You just want to tell the browser "I want an image here".

This type of tag also ends with a slash "/", but this time the slash is at the end of the tag.

Example:

```
<siteraw />
```

Note that since HTML5, the use of ending slashes "/" for standalone tags is in no way compulsory. You could very well write <siteraw />, <siteraw/> or <siteraw>.

I recommend to always add the slash. First because it provides a visual clue that allows you to instantly identify paired tags and standalone tags. And second because it's good programming practice to do so, as it is required in most markup languages (XML, xHTML...).

The space before the slash is always optional.

HTML ATTRIBUTES

Now that you know about HTML tags, let's talk about their attributes. I say "their" attributes, because as you'll see HTML attributes always accompany HTML tags (the reverse isn't true as you can have tags with no attributes).

Just like tags, attributes are used to transmit information to the browser. But where tags send instructions about either the web page or elements thereof, attributes give information about the tags they belong to.

There are two components of an HTML attribute: the **name** and the **value**.

Here is how they are used.

```
<website name="SiteRaw" />
```

We have our HTML tag <website /> (a standalone tag ~~for retards~~ if you've already forgotten), and one attribute. Our attribute has the very creative name "*name*" and the value "*SiteRaw*".

You aren't limited to just one attribute per tag. An HTML tag can have as many attributes as you want.

```
<website name="SiteRaw" type="website" />
```

One, two, three, ten or even zero. You can add as many attributes as you want.

But what about paired tags? Do they also have attributes?

Yes.

In the case of paired tags, the attributes are only placed in the opening tag and not the closing tag.

Going back to our previous example.

```
<website name="SiteRaw">SiteRaw</website>
```

Some HTML tags share attributes between each other, others have attributes designed strictly for their use. As I mentioned, none of these tags or attributes are real. Remember the principles, not the actual (stupid) examples.

 You may have seen attributes with a name but no value, in the format `<tag attribute />`. If there is no visible value, it's because the attribute takes a default value if none is specified. These cases are rare and there are usually only a few choices of values, such as a Boolean (true or false).

PROPER HTML TAG PRACTICES

View the source code of any website, even those professionally designed, and you're bound to see the same errors appear again and again. These mistakes are often bad habits picked up when learn to code that have stuck around due to lack of clarification. Throughout this course we will see the proper habits to acquire to produce semantically correct HTML code. In addition, I will also highlight the most common instances of bad HTML practices.

Here are two unfortunately common examples.

UNCLOSED TAGS

As we saw in the last section, writing a standalone tag as either `<tag />`, `<tag/>` or `<tag>` makes very little difference (although I advise against the last syntax).

But if you're using paired tags, don't forget to close them!

Not only is it required for semantically valid HTML, but having missing closing tags can seriously mess up the way your web page is rendered by the browser as it won't know where one element start and another ends, and which parts of each element belong to which tag.

- **BAD:** <del><siteraw>Hello World!</del>
- **GOOD:** <siteraw>Hello World!</siteraw>

OVERLAPPING TAGS

When we use several HTML tags simultaneously (inevitable), say <siteraw> and <website> from one of our previous examples, it is imperative to respect the hierarchy of tags: the first one to open is the last one to close.

Having intertwined tags is an incorrect practice.

- **BAD:** <del><website>Welcome to <siteraw>SiteRaw</website></siteraw></del>
- **GOOD:** <website>Welcome to <siteraw>SiteRaw</siteraw></website>

THE STRUCTURE OF AN HTML PAGE

Let's start building our first true web page. From now on we will use real HTML tags and attributes.

Open your text editor and write the following code.

```
<!DOCTYPE html>
<html>
    <head>
        <meta charset="utf-8" />
        <title>SiteRaw</title>
    </head>

    <body>


    </body>
</html>
```

I added spaces at the start of some lines to make the code more readable. This practice is called indentation and has no effect on how the page is rendered, it only serves to make your code easier on the eye.

You can get the same result by pressing the Tab key before each line.

This is what you should get in your text editor.

The foundation of your HTML page

Remember the rule about using multiple HTML tags synchronously? To avoid overlaps, the first tag to open is the last tag to close.

 What are all these tags and what do they do?

As mentioned just above, from now on we will be using real HTML tags and attributes. The code I gave you can be considered the starting point or the blueprint for any web page. In other words, this is the minimal code you will need to include to produce a semantically valid HTML document (a web page).

Here is a detailed explanation of every element on this page, one line at a time.

THE DOCTYPE

Remember when I said that everything in an HTML document is either a tag or included in at least one tag? A doctype, short for document type declaration, is not an actual HTML tag (it's the lone exception that confirms the rule).

```
<!DOCTYPE html>
```

The doctype is an instruction that associates a specific markup document (in our case, a web page) with a document type definition (DTD).

In short, it tells the web browser what type of document it's accessing. For us it will be an HTML web page. There are many types of doctypes and some can get rather long and complicated. Luckily, HTML5 doctypes are very short and easy to remember. This wasn't always the case when building websites.

As a rule, the first line of your web page will always be reserved for the doctype.

THE HTML TAG

Next comes the `<html>` tag.

This tags encloses the entire HTML document. Everything except the doctype is placed within this tag.

```
<html> [...] </html>
```

As you can see, there is nothing after the last `</html>`.

THE HEADER AND BODY

A web page is divided in two essential components:

- The **header** (<head>), which contains information that is not usually rendered by the browser.
- The **body** (<body>), which is where the main content of your web page will be located.

Save for the doctype, any content present on your web page should be included in either the <head> or <body> tags, which are themselves includes in the <html> tag.

META TAGS

Meta tags (plural) are invariably included in the header of your web page. These tags describe the metadata of your document.

If you want a concrete example, meta elements are typically used to specify a web page's description, keywords, author, the date last modified and so forth. There are quite a lot of meta tags in the HTML language, most of which vary between circumstantially practical and completely useless.

However, I did include one in our blueprint: the charset.

```
<meta charset="utf-8" />
```

The **charset**, short for character set, is the encoding of your document. It specifies to the web browser how special characters, such as symbols, accents or non-Latin characters, are to be displayed.

There are many forms of character encoding, usually with incomprehensible names such as *ISO-8859-1* or *Windows-1253*. I suggest you always use *UTF-8*. This encoding method allows you to display almost every character you can think of, without having to modify your page's encoding each time.

This is the charset I include in our blueprint.

The charset meta tag does not modify the encoding of your file. It simply helps the browser determine what character set your page is using. Brackets automatically saves your files in UTF-8, but for other text editors you need to specify your character set. With Sublime Text for instance, you need to go to File > Save with Encoding > UTF-8 to encode your document in UTF-8. If you get any errors while trying to display accents, make sure the character set in the meta tag matches the encoding of your document.

THE TITLE TAG

The title tag contains, unsurprisingly, the title of your web page. In our demo the title is "SiteRaw", but it's up to you to modify it and give you page a more relevant name.

It's advisable to keep the title fairly short with no more than 120 characters.

```
<title>SiteRaw</title>
```

As with most header tags, the content of your title tag doesn't appear on your web page. It is nonetheless a very important tag. For example, most browsers will show the text contained within your title tag at the top of each page, usually in a browser tab.

In addition, the content of your title tag will be displayed in search results on most search engines.

Your page title appears in search results

That concludes our review of the basic HTML tags. You are free to edit your demo page as much as you want, just make sure that your code follows the model. This blueprint should be the backbone of every page you create as it contains every essential HTML component.

 But... my web page is empty :(I opened it with my browser and it just shows a blank page!

HTML COMMENTS

Before concluding this chapter and moving on to building your website, let's talk a bit about HTML comments. A comment in HTML is information you write for you, the web developer. Think of it as a memo or a bookmark. Comments are not rendered, they are not read by the browser and they do not alter the display of the page.

 So they're useless?

Somewhat.

But they do come in handy. You can use comments to document your code, mark guidelines if your page is very large, or even leave indications on what purpose each elements serves in case you forget after a while.

HOW TO INSERT A COMMENT

To write a comment in HTML, you simply wrap the text you want around two markers: `<!--` and `-->`.

For example:

```
<!-- This is a comment -->
```

You can add comments wherever you want in your page. To go back to our demo page:

```
<!DOCTYPE html>
<html>
    <head> <!-- Header -->
        <meta charset="utf-8" />
        <title>SiteRaw</title>
    </head>

    <body> <!-- Body -->

    </body>
</html>
```

As I said, comments are ignored by the browser. There is no difference in display between this code and the commentless one above.

Comments are not used very often in HTML but I wanted to show them to you so you're not surprised if you see them from time to time. I will occasionally use them within my examples to remind you of certain guidelines or to give you a quick explanation without interruption the code.

HOW TO VIEW THE SOURCE CODE

HTML comments differ from those of most computer languages. In general, comments are annotations that are readable by the developer or developers but disappear once the program is compiled or interpreted. As such, they don't appear in the end product.

Not so in HTML.

The reason is simple: HTML pages aren't compiled or interpreted, they are simply sent "as is" to the web browser. What that means is that once your website is online, anyone who visits it can see your comments... and not just your comments either, anyone who access your website can view the source code. The term source code is just a fancy name for the HTML code of your web page.

Try it for yourself.

Right-click anywhere on a page and select `View Page Source`. Most browsers have this function in the right click drop-down menu, although the exact text may vary.

That's the HTML code that gave you the web page you're currently browsing.

ORGANIZE YOUR TEXT WITH HTML

O k, so the blank page is nice and all but your website isn't likely to be very successful if you leave things as they are. The first step to "fill" your site is to give it some content. The easiest and most common way being by writing text inside the `<body>` tag we mentioned last chapter. We'll see that having your HTML page display textual content is in fact very simple as HTML allows you to arrange whatever type of text you can imagine.

In this chapter, you'll learn:

- how to structure your text in paragraphs
- how to organize your page with different titles
- how to emphasize and highlight certain words
- how to insert different kinds of lists

Let's start building our website.

PARAGRAPHS

You want to add text to your web page but don't know how? In HTML, things are rather simple: text content is placed within **paragraphs**.

Paragraphs are delineated by the <p> tag (p is for paragraph).

```
<p>This is my paragraph.</p>
```

As you can see, <p> is a paired tag.

- <p> indicates the beginning of the paragraph
- </p> marks the end of the paragraph

Paragraphs go in the <body> section of your HTML page, which as we learned last chapter is reserved for the visible elements destined to be rendered (as opposed to the invisible ones which go in the <head>).

All that's left to do is take the code of our demo page and add a paragraph.

```
<!DOCTYPE html>
<html>
    <head>
        <meta charset="utf-8" />
        <title>SiteRaw</title>
    </head>

    <body>

        <p>Welcome to SiteRaw.</p>

    </body>
</html>
```

Try it and see the result for yourself. Feel free to modify the text as you wish. You can even add another paragraph following the first one, there are no limits as to their number in an HTML page. In fact, let's try it out.

Copy and paste the following code in your text editor.

```
<!DOCTYPE html>
<html>
    <head>
        <meta charset="utf-8" />
        <title>SiteRaw</title>
    </head>

    <body>

        <p>This is my first paragraph.</p>

        <p>This is my second paragraph.
    Read it well!</p>

    </body>
</html>
```

It's not Homeric poetry, but it's pretty good nonetheless.

 But... in the second paragraph it's supposed to go to a new line... instead everything is on the same line! It doesn't work!

I see what you mean.

You were probably expecting to see something to the extent of:

```
This is my second paragraph.
Read it well!
```

Instead you got:

```
This is my second paragraph. Read it well!
```

It's perfectly normal.

We need to tell the browser that we want a new line. In HTML, line breaks work a bit differently than you're used to.

LINE BREAKS IN HTML

If you've commonly used word processors such as Microsoft Word in the past, you're already familiar with line breaks.

A **line break**, also called carriage-return, is simply an indication to start a new line. It's not as pronounced as a paragraph, it simply marks the end of a line and the start of a new one. In most word processors, to create a new line you simply hit the Enter key. Obviously things aren't so simple in HTML as you've just experienced.

To mark a line break in HTML you simply use the <br /> tag. It's a standalone tag, meaning there is no closing tag and it doesn't hold any content.

Going back to our example:

```
<!DOCTYPE html>
<html>
    <head>
        <meta charset="utf-8" />
        <title>SiteRaw</title>
    </head>

    <body>

        <p>This is my first paragraph.</p>

        <p>This is my second paragraph.<br />
Read it well!</p>

    </body>
</html>
```

Now everything works perfectly.

Understood?

- <p> and </p> tags are for paragraphs.
- the <br /> tag is for line breaks.

Since we finally got our paragraphs to work as we wanted, let's add some titles.

TITLES

Once we start adding more content to our web page, things might get a little difficult to read. Titles are useful to organize your text in distinct segments.

And with HTML, we're quite lucky... we have not one but six different choices of title tags.

Don't be scared by the number, all these tags follow the same rules and in fact they can be grouped in one big supra-tag: <hX>, where X is a number between 1 and 6.

Why six tags?

They are used to indicate the level of importance of a title.

Here is how they work:

- `<h1>` means "very important title". Usually there is only one per page although this is just convention.
- `<h2>` means "important title".
- `<h3>` means "somewhat important title".
- `<h4>` means "somewhat lesser title".
- `<h5>` means "lesser title".
- `<h6>` means "least important title".

You don't need to use every single level of title on each web page.

I recommend you start with `<h1>`. Then, if you need to make a sub-title, use one or more `<h2>` tags. If you need sub-subtitles, use `<h3>` and so on.

 But I thought we already had a title tag in HTML.

True.

Last chapter we introduced the `<title>` tag, which goes in the `<head>` portion of your code.

These tags are actually called **headers** (h is for header).

You also said there was a header tag already!

Look, I didn't invent these names.

Just don't confuse the following:

- <head> is the header tag, as opposed to the body tag (<body>). These two go in the <html> tag.
- <title> is the title of your web page, it goes in the header (<head>, see above).
- <h1> to <h6> are called whatever you want. Some call them titles, others call them headers, some even call them "h" tags. They go in the body (<body>) of your web page.

Nomenclature isn't that important.

What is critical is that you don't confuse them and start using one in place of the other.

Let's try adding these tags to our demo page.

```
<!DOCTYPE html>
<html>
    <head>
        <meta charset="utf-8" />
        <title>SiteRaw</title>
    </head>

    <body>

      <h1>Welcome to SiteRaw</h1>

        <p>The best site on the interwebz.</p>

        <h2>Free tutorials for beginners</h2>

        <p>This is my second paragraph.</p>

        <p>(ok I ran out of ideas... try to do
better)</p>

    </body>
</html>
```

This is how things should look in your text editor.

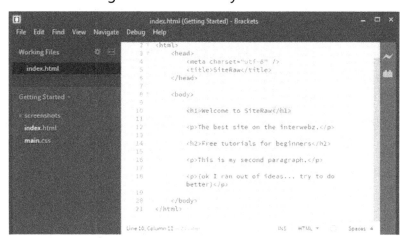

HTML page with titles

Try it out.

Now we have something that's beginning to look like a real web page.

 *You might have noticed that the render of **<h1>** tags in the browser is larger than that of **<h2>** tags, which in turn is larger than **<h3>** and so on. Don't choose your title tags based on the size of the rendered text. These title tags are important for hierarchical structure, aesthetic display is secondary and can be modified using CSS (we will see how further on in this tutorial). It's entirely possible to make **<h3>** titles larger than **<h1>** in CSS, but the order of importance can't be changed.*

HIGHLIGHTS

We saw how to structure our web page in paragraphs and organize it using titles. But what about putting emphasis on some words or sentences within a paragraph? The HTML language provides you with many ways of highlighting parts of your text.

EMPHASIS

Adding emphasis to your text is very easy to do in HTML. All you need is to enclose the text you want to put emphasis on inside the emphasis tag: <em>.

Here is an example of how emphasis works:

```
<p>Welcome to <em>SiteRaw</em>, the best
website ever!</p>
```

And the result:

Welcome to *SiteRaw*, the best website ever!

As you can see, the emphasized text is now written in italics.

This is simply something the browser does to make the text stand out. You will be able to modify it later using CSS.

STRONG EMPHASIS

The emphasis tag is too weak for your taste? You want something really brutal? Good for you, there is another tag to indicate emphasis on your text called the strong emphasis tag.

Just like with regular emphasis, all you need is to enclose your selected text within the strong emphasis tag: <strong>.

Here is our example:

```
<p>Welcome to <strong>SiteRaw</strong>, the
best website ever!</p>
```

And the result:

Welcome to **SiteRaw**, the best website ever!

Once again you can see that the browser took the liberty of rendering your emphasized text in bold to make it stand out.

It's a default behavior that is easily modified in CSS.

 Is there any difference between emphasis with the <em> tag and strong emphasis with the <strong> tag?

Honestly, no.

They are completely interchangeable and serve the exact same purpose. While the official position is that one is "strong" emphasis and the other is "regular" emphasis, apparently no one has taken the time to define what either of those two adjectives mean.

Use whichever you want, or both.

Mark Highlights

There is a third way to highlight text in HTML. The marked text tag is used to make an extract stand out from the rest of your text. It can be used to highlight relevant text in a list of search results for example.

Its application is identical to the two previous tags, just remember to used the marked text tag: <mark>.

For example:

```
<p>Welcome to <mark>SiteRaw</mark>, the
best website ever!</p>
```

And the result:

```
Welcome to SiteRaw, the best website ever!
```

By default, the text is highlighted in yellow.

This is once again completely adjustable so don't worry too much about the visual effects.

Rare but sometimes useful tags

There are few additional tags that you won't use very often

to say the least, but that might prove practical at some point or another. Maybe.

You don't have to remember these, just think of this section as a bonus.

- **Inserted text:** Use the `<ins>` tag.
- **Deleted text:** Use the `<del>` tag.
- **Keyboard input:** Use the `<kbd>` tag.
- **Quotes:** Use the `<q>` tag.
- **Code:** Use the `<code>` tag.
- **Superscript:** Use the `<sup>` tag.
- **Subscript:** Use the `<sub>` tag.
- **Small print:** Use the `<small>` tag.

Good luck finding use for all of them.

HTML FOR CONTENT, CSS FOR STYLE

It bears repeating that `<strong>`, `<em>` and `<mark>` are not formatting tags.

Many beginners see these tags and say to themselves: "Great! Now I know how to bolden, italicize and mark my text in HTML". This is a common mistake, made by by beginners and long time web developers alike. Every tag in HTML has a meaning beyond its cosmetic appearance. In fact, HTML is not used for appearance at all.

If you want bold, italic, underline, over-line (yes, it's a thing), pink blinking text or whatever else you can imagine, wait until we learn CSS.

You can even make the `<em>` tag bold and the `<strong>` tag italic if you want.

The golden rule of web development is as follows: HTML for the content, CSS for the style.

LIST TAGS

You thought this chapter was over?

Think again, we still have one more HTML constituent to cover: the list element.

HTML lists are very common and extremely practical when it comes to organizing information in a readable way.

I will introduce two types of lists:

- bulleted lists, also called unordered lists
- numbered lists, also called ordered lists

We will start with bulleted lists, the most common occurrence.

Bulleted lists

You've probably seen many bulleted lists already, not least in this chapter.

Here is what bulleted lists looks like:

- Welcome
- to
- SiteRaw

This is a practical system as it allows you to create a list of items absent of hierarchical order, as opposed to the numbered list which we'll present further on.

These lists are very easy to create in HTML, the only point you need to remember is that you need two HTML tags to create such a list. Why two? You'll understand in a moment.

When we visualize a list, we think of one unique element.

Instead, consider that there are two components to a list: the **list itself** and each **individual item**.

In HTML, you need to instruct the browser where the list starts and ends as well as where each bullet point starts and ends.

So here are the two tags you need:

- <ul> indicates where the list starts and ends (stands for Unordered List)
- <li> indicates where each item starts and ends (stands for List Item)

The <li> tags are naturally place inside the <ul> tag.

Here is the HTML code for the example I gave above.

```
<ul>
    <li>Welcome</li>
    <li>to</li>
    <li>SiteRaw</li>
</ul>
```

You can add as many items as you want.

You can even create bulleted lists within other bulleted lists. These are called nested lists.

All you have to do is open a new list (with <ul>) within an item from the first list (<li>).

Here is a demonstration.

```
<ul>
    <li>SiteRaw</li>
    <li>is
        <ul>
            <li>awesome</li>
            <li>a website</li>
            <li>SiteRaw (no s...)</li>
        </ul>
    </li>
</ul>
```

This code gives you:

- SiteRaw
- is
    - awesome
    - a website
    - SiteRaw (no s...)

Just remember to close the tags in the right order.

*Every HTML element has a default display value, most of the time either **block** or **inline**. With the notable exception of the <p> tag (for paragraphs), every tag we saw up until now is an inline element. The <ul> tag (for unordered lists) however is a block element. In summary, a block element starts on a new line and always takes up the full width available, whereas an inline element doesn't require a new line and only takes up as much width as necessary. Since both <p> and <ul> are both block elements, you don't need to include your lists inside paragraphs.*

NUMBERED LISTS

The second type of list we will discover is the numbered list.

Though slightly less prevalent than bulleted lists, they are nonetheless used quite often in HTML pages.

Here is what they look like:

1. Welcome
2. to
3. SiteRaw

Numbered lists work in the exact same way as bulleted lists.

The only difference is that you have to indicate in your code that you want an ordered list (`<ol>`) rather than an unordered list (`<ul>`).

Nothing changes within the list: we still use `<li>` to delineate the beginning and end of an item.

 The order in which you place your items is important. The first entry will correspond to item number one, the second to item number two and so on.

Here is the code of our example:

```
<ol>
    <li>Welcome</li>
    <li>to</li>
    <li>SiteRaw</li>
</ol>
```

As you can see, the only difference between the bulleted list and the numbered list is the HTML tag used to insert them.

- `<ul>` is for bulleted lists (Unordered List)
- `<ol>` is for numbered lists (Ordered List)
- `<li>` is for each entry, independent of the type of list used (List Item)

Now that you know how to create paragraphs, insert line breaks, incorporate titles, add highlights and manipulate lists, let's try updating our demo page with our newfound knowledge.

Here is our complete HTML code.

```
<!DOCTYPE html>
<html>
    <head>
        <meta charset="utf-8" />
        <title>SiteRaw</title>
    </head>

    <body>
```

```
<h1>Welcome to SiteRaw</h1>

<p>The <strong>best site</strong> on
the interwebz.</p>

<h2>Why is SiteRaw so awesome?</h2>

<p>Here are a few reasons:</p>

<ul>
   <li>because it's SiteRaw</li>
   <li>because it's awesome</li>
   <li>because reasons</li>
</ul>

   </body>
 </html>
```

This is just my demonstration, you can of course use whatever tags you want from those we just learned. And feel free to amend the nonsensical text to make it more relevant to your website.

As you can see, the list tags are placed either before, between or after the paragraphs, not inside. That has to do with the default display behavior of <p> and <ul>/<ol>, both behind block elements as opposed to inline elements such as <strong>.

This chapter covered a lot of new HTML tags and your web page should now start to take form.

But it's not a real website yet as there is still something missing.

Keep reading and we'll find out what in the next chapter.

CREATE TEXT LINKS

In the previous chapter, we learned how to build a basic HTML page. But a website is more than a single HTML page. You could make the point that what defines a website is the presence of a collection of related web pages. Get that? Multiple web pages. And how does one go from one web page to the other? Through **hypertext links** of course.

You click on a certain piece of text and you're magically transported to another page. It's no exaggeration to say that hyperlinks are the backbone of a website. Luckily, creating text links is a standard and easy to learn HTML practice. There are two types of text links in HTML and we'll cover them both in this chapter.

You can create a link from page `a.html` to page `b.html` (relative link) but you can also create a link to a completely different website such as `http://www.siteraw.com` (absolute link).

Both work in a very similar fashion.

RELATIVE OR ABSOLUTE?

As I briefly mentioned in this chapter's introduction, there are two types of links:

- **Relative links** are links internal to one's own website, pointing for example from page `a.html` to page `b.html`.
- **Absolute links** are links to an external site, pointing for example to `http://www.siteraw.com`.

Remember the distinction between absolute and relative as these terms are used for more than just text links. Each time you have to deal with paths and the file system, you can bet that you'll encounter the relative/absolute dichotomy.

 To get a bit technical, while true, my explanation isn't necessarily the most accurate. The terms relative and absolute refer to the path of a file or directory rather than the location of the destination. As such, it's possible to create absolute links pointing to internal pages of your website.

Ready to start creating links?

ABSOLUTE LINKS

Let's start with absolute links. It's easy to recognize a hypertext link on most web pages as they are intentionally formatted to stand out from the rest of the text (in blue and underlined by default).

Let's append a link to the demo page we built during the last chapter.

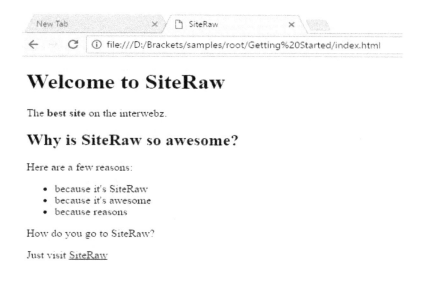

Remember this?

You can see the link in blue at the bottom of the page.

So how do we insert hyperlinks in HTML?

All we need to create links in HTML is one tag: <a>.

The <a> stands for anchor, which we'll talk about in a few moments, but it's mostly known as the hyperlink tag. To insert a link on your page, simply enter the text you want to transform into a link between the <a> tags.

In our case the linked text in "SiteRaw".

```
<a>SiteRaw</a>
```

Feel free to change the text if you want.

 It doesn't work! When I click on the link nothing happens!

That's because we haven't specified the destination of our link yet. If you think about it, a link needs to have at least two components: the **element linked** (in our case the text "SiteRaw") and the **link destination** (what we need to add).

To do that we'll use a specific HTML attribute.

Remember attributes? We introduced them in the second chapter but haven't used them since.

The attribute we need to indicate the destination of our link is href, which stands for <u>hypertext reference</u>. And don't forget the rule for using attributes: they are placed on the opening tag and not on the closing tag.

Let's complete our link by adding a href attribute and having our text point to http://www.siteraw.com.

```
<a href="http://www.siteraw.com">SiteRaw</a>
```

Links should should generally be used in paragraphs so we're going to add some text around it.

```
<p>Just visit <a href="http://www.siteraw.
com">SiteRaw</a></p>
```

And that's the exact code used for the example given at the beginning of this chapter.

Let's move on to relative links.

RELATIVE LINKS

We learned how to link to an existing website, now all we need is to be able to create links between the pages of our own site.

To do this we will be using relative links.

 How can I create links between my pages if I don't know the web address of my website? I don't have a http:// address yet!

Don't worry, you can still use links even without having a web address. Your website is currently stored on your computer and only you can see it. We'll discover how to send it online and make it accessible to everyone in the world further on in this tutorial.

But for the moment we'll make do with what we have. Over the course of this tutorial we've created one HTML page (called index.html or whatever else you named it). As we said in the introduction, to qualify as a complete website you need at least two pages so we're just going to create another page in the same directory. I called it siteraw.html.

In Brackets, just go to File > New and save your new file in the same folder as your first page.

Here is what you should have in your file explorer.

Two HTML pages in the same directory

All that's left to do is create a link from `index.html` to `siteraw.html`.

But how can I do that if I don't know the `http://` address?

Very easily.

Since both files are in the same directory, just take the code we used in our previous example and replace the value of the `href` attribute by `siteraw.html` (the name of your destination page).

Whatever names you use for your HTML files, one page will be the linking page and the other will be the destination page.

In our case, `index.html` will be linking to `siteraw.html`.

Here is the code for `index.html`.

```
<p>Want to visit <a href="siteraw.html">SiteRaw
</a>? It's an awesome website!</p>
```

And the code for `siteraw.html`.

```
<h1>Welcome to SiteRaw</h1>
```

The linking page (`index.html`) contains a link to the destination page (`siteraw.html`) which simply consists of a message indicating that you've arrived on the right page.

Try it out.

 To shorten the code I intentionally omitted the usual structure tags (<html>, <head>, <body> and so on), but you should always include them for your web pages to be valid.

PAGES IN DIFFERENT FOLDERS

Now you know how to create relative links. Or do you? There are still one or two points to cover.

Yes, you only showed how to create relative links when the two files are in the same folder. What if they're not?

Good point.

Things are slightly more difficult when your pages are in different folders but it's still quite simple. Let's revise our example and imagine that rather than being in the same directory as `index.html`, the page `siteraw.html` is in a folder called `siteraw`.

I know I'm very creative with my appellations so here's a visual aid.

The siteraw.html file is located in the siteraw folder

Inside the `siteraw` folder is the same file `siteraw.html` as before, its content hasn't changed. So how do we create a link from `index.html` to `siteraw.html`?

Just add the name of the folder before the name of the file in the `href` attribute.

```
<a href="siteraw/siteraw.html">SiteRaw</a>
```

And what if there were several folders separating them? Instead of having to go `siteraw` > `siteraw.html`, what if you had to go `siteraw` > `folder` > `siteraw.html`?

Same method, just add the names of the folders separated by slashes.

```
<a href="siteraw/folder/siteraw.html">SiteRaw</a>
```

 Ok, but what if the destination page isn't located in a sub-folder but in a parent directory?

If your destination page is placed "higher" in the tree structure, simply write two dots `..` for each directory you want to "climb".

```
<a href="../siteraw.html">SiteRaw</a>
```

We've now seen both types of links, absolute and relative, and learned how to operate them with HTML.

But there is still one more practice to learn about.

LINKING TO ANCHORS

At the beginning of this chapter I told you the <a> tag stood for "anchor". Although it's used far more often to create hyperlinks, we're about to introduce an alternative use of this HTML tag.

 So what are anchors?

An anchor is a reference point you place somewhere on your page that allows the user to jump directly to the desired content. Think of it as the unofficial third type of link, a link to content within the same page.

Anchors are useful when your page is very long and you want to organize it in a way that provides rapid access to the user.

To create an anchor we first need to create an anchor point, and for that we'll use the attribute id. The anchor point is the area on which the visitor will land once he clicks a specific link on the page.

You can place the id attribute wherever you want: on a <p> (paragraph), on a <ul> (list) or on a <h2> (title).

The id attribute is a rare case in HTML to the extent that it can be placed on any tag you want. If an HTML tag exists, you can be sure it can hold an id attribute. The only restriction is that no two tags can have share the same id They must be unique.

In our example we will go with the the title tags.

```
<h2 id="siteraw">Welcome to SiteRaw</h2>
```

I used the value "siteraw" for the id attribute but you can change it to something else. The only rule is that every id must be unique.

Now that we created our anchor point all that's left is to add a link to it. These anchor links are identical to regular links except that their href attribute doesn't point to another page but to the id of an anchor point, preceded by a hash character (#).

In our case it would give us the following.

```
<a href="#siteraw">Go to the SiteRaw anchor</a>
```

Just place the link anywhere above the anchor and you can now travel directly to the content you want.

 It doesn't work! Nothing happens when I click on a link.

That's because you haven't added enough text between the link and the anchor.

Here is our demo page updated with anchor links.

```
<!DOCTYPE html>
<html>
    <head>
        <meta charset="utf-8" />
        <title>SiteRaw</title>
    </head>

    <body>
    <h1>Welcome to SiteRaw</h1>

        <p>Discover why SiteRaw is:</p>

        <ul>
            <li><a href="#awesome">awesome</a></li>
            <li><a href="#amazing">amazing</a></li>
            <li><a href="#siteraw">SiteRaw</a></li>
        </ul>
        <!-- Remember lists? -->

        <h2 id="awesome">Why SiteRaw is
```

93

```
awesome</h2>

        <p>[...]</p>

        <h2 id="amazing">Why SiteRaw is
amazing</h2>

        <p>[...]</p>

        <h2 id="siteraw">Why SiteRaw is
SiteRaw</h2>

        <p>[...]</p>

    </body>
</html>
```

Replace every instance of [...] with (a lot of) text and you should see the effect in action.

You will have to add a sufficient amount of content to see the vertical scroll bars appear on your browser, so depending on your screen resolution you may need more or less text. Usually more. Alternatively, you can reduce the size of your browser window to make the scroll bars appear.

Here is what your text editor should look like at the moment.

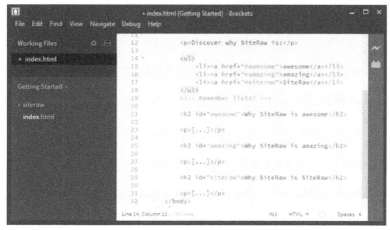

HTML page with titles

ANCHORS ON ANOTHER PAGE

As we saw, anchors are useful to navigate quickly to a specific section of a web page. But you can also use them in conjunction with regular links.

The idea is to have a link that opens another page and takes you directly to an anchor on that new page. To do this just enter the name of the destination page followed by the name of the anchor with the hash character (#) in front of it.

```
<a href="siteraw.html#siteraw">SiteRaw</a>
```

This link will take you to the page siteraw.html and to the anchor called siteraw.

These are the three types of links we discovered in this chapter:

- **Absolute links** which point to another site
- **Relative links** which point to a page on our site
- **Anchor links** which point to specific content

Since we know how to create multiple pages and link them together, we now officially have a complete website.

But don't worry as there is much more to learn about in this tutorial.

INSERT IMAGES

Now that we have an almost complete website, what could possibly be left to cover in this tutorial? Quite a lot, actually. For starters let's talk about images. Inserting an image in a web page is surprisingly easy, but there are nevertheless a few details to consider.

The format of your image is one of them. Not all images are created equal and depending on which format you choose, you may trade quality for compression or vice-versa. Images are quite heavy in terms of file size, much more so than text, so larger images mean slower loading time.

We'll start this chapter by introducing different image formats and determining which one is best suited for each specific need.

Keep reading to find out more.

DIFFERENT IMAGE FORMATS

Image formats are means of storing the digital data of a computer image. Depending on which formats your file is stored in, your image will be more or less compressed which will in turn affect the quality and the size of your file.

You've probably seen image file formats before.

For example, Adobe Photoshop allows you to choose between different formats when you save an image.

Image formats provided by Photoshop

As you can see you have more than enough choice as of which image format to use on your website. We are going to cover the three main file formats used for displaying images on web pages. These are the three types of images you will run into most often.

They all share one point in common: they are compressed, meaning that they are optimized for faster loading on web pages.

THE JPEG FORMAT

The **JPEG format** stands for "Joint Photographic Expert Group" and, as you may have guessed from its name, is particularly common in the field of digital photography. But that's far from its only use. The JPEG compression method is very advantageous when creating or adapting images for their use on web media.

This format is specifically designed to reduce the size of large photos in order to optimize their loading speed.

The following is a photo saved under the JPEG format.

A JPEG photograph

JPEG images are saved with the file extension `.jpg` or less frequently `.jpeg`. Note that JPEG is a lossy compression method, so depending on the amount of compression you choose you may see a slight though generally imperceptible drop in image quality. This is what makes it possible to store large photos at reduced file sizes. It's usually very hard to detect a loss in quality via naked eye unless you've overly compressed your file.

With some types of images however, I'm tempted to say anything that's not a photograph, the image may appear to be slightly blurry. In that case it's better to use another image format such as PNG.

THE PNG FORMAT

The **PNG format** stands for "Portable Graphic Network" and is a relatively modern image system. This format is most suited for most graphics and particularly for computer generated images.

Compared to JPEG, the PNG image format excels when the image possesses large, uniformly colored areas. Basically anything that's not a photo.

The following is an image saved in the PNG format. You may recognize it from somewhere.

The SiteRaw logo saved in PNG

PNG is a lossless compression method, meaning that while the image is naturally optimized the compression process doesn't affect the image quality. The PNG image format boasts another advantage: it supports transparent images.

 If PNG images have better quality and can supports transparency, what's the point of JPEG?

The JPEG format has better compression.

For large files, an image saved in JPEG will almost always load faster than one saved in PNG. I recommend using JPEG essentially for photos of considerable size and for images whose loading speed you want to optimize at the expense of absolute quality.

THE GIF FORMAT

The **GIF format** stands for Graphics Interchange Format. You've most likely already heard of it, as the name has become nearly synonymous with its main feature: the ability to display animated images.

GIF images are limited to 256 colors but, just like with the PNG format, they support transparency.

The following image is saved under the GIF format.

An animated GIF image

These are the three most used formats on the web.

THE BEST FORMAT FOR YOUR IMAGE

There isn't a universal best format for your image.

Rather, there are different formats that exist to achieve separate needs.

- The JPEG format is best used for photos
- The PNG format is best used for graphics
- The GIF format is best used for animated images

As mentioned above, these are the three most commonly used image formats for web development.

 What about other formats such as TIFF (.tif) or BITMAP (.bmp)?

The formats not presented here are usually not adapted for web usage, mainly because they are often not compressed and therefore too big to load on a web page.

INSERTING AN IMAGE

Let's get back to our HTML code.

All you need to insert an image in a web page is the `<img />` tag. As you may have guessed, it stands for "image". This is a standalone tag. You might remember the distinction from the second chapter of this tutorial. Standalone tags such as `<img />` or `<br />` don't need to be opened and closed and as such you don't need to enter two tags as was the case with most other HTML elements we have seen so far.

It can carry two attributes, which are mandatory.

They are the following:

- **src** stands for "source" and indicates the location of the image file you want to insert. It can be included either through a relative path (e.g. `images/siteraw.png`) or through an absolute one (e.g. `http://www.siteraw.com/siteraw.png`), the first being a much more common practice. Refer to last chapter's introduction to links if you forgot what absolute and relative mean.
- **alt** stands for "alternative text" and is a short description of the image. This tag doesn't seem like it's very useful at first sight, but it must always be included. Every image needs an alternative text. Many agents such as search engine robots and non-visual browsers (those of blind web surfers in particular) need an alternative text to know what the image is about. Additionally, this is text that will appear if the image can't be loaded on your page for any reason.

Images are by default inline elements (they don't create a new line on a page) so they must be included in block-level tags. In our case, we'll include our image inside paragraph (<p>) tags. It's the only block element we know of for the moment.

Here is our HTML code.

```
<p>
    Welcome to SiteRaw.<br />
    <img src="images/siteraw.jpg" alt="SiteRaw
Logo" />
</p>
```

And... that's it.

Inserting images is ludicrously simple in HTML. The only "difficult" part is choosing the right format.

ALTERNATIVE TEXT

As we've briefly mentioned, the alternative text attribute (alt) specifies an alternate text for the image in case it can't be loaded. This is not only important if the image fails to load, in case of a slow connection or an error in the src attribute, but it's also necessary for proper indexation by search engines and their robots.

Since HTML5 this attribute is no longer strictly required for a semantically valid page but you should nevertheless always supply your images with an alternative text for the reasons mentioned above.

Browsers for visually impaired users will read the text aloud while text browsers will always show the alternative text instead of the image. Search engine robots will not download the image to try and figure out what it is and if it has relevance to your web page. Instead, they will simply read the `alt` attribute to determine what the image is about. Some very old browsers also display the content of the `alt` attribute as a tooltip but that shouldn't be the case with modern versions. Speaking of which, how do you display a tooltip?

ADDING A TOOLTIP

The attribute used to display a visual tooltip on the hover of the mouse is `title`. Unlike `alt`, this attribute is completely optional.

The `title` attribute belongs to what are called global attributes. These are attributes common to all HTML elements. As such you aren't limited to using `title` on an image, you can apply it to a paragraph, a link or even an emphasis. We mentioned another global attribute previously, do you remember it? It was `id` which is applicable to every HTML tag.

Here is an example.

```
<img src="siteraw.png" alt="SiteRaw Logo"
title="The Logo of SiteRaw" />
```

Hover your mouse pointer over the image to see the tooltip appear.

A CLICKABLE IMAGE

Just as you can create a text link (see last chapter), you can also create a clickable image link. Instead of placing textual content between the <a> elements, simply place an image (<img />) tag.

Here is the HTML code.

```
<p>
    Want to visit an awesome website? Click the
image below!<br />
    <a href="http://www.siteraw.com"><img
src="siteraw.png" alt="Visit SiteRaw!" /></a>
</p>
```

And there you have a clickable image.

 Some browsers will show a somewhat visually unsightly blue or purple border around image links. We can easily remove this frame in CSS so don't mind it if it does appear on your browser.

FIGURES

Throughout this tutorial you've frequently come across figures. Figures are HTML elements that represent self-contained content and enhance the text by supplementing information on the page. Contrary to popular belief, figures aren't necessarily images. Although images are often the preferred format, figures can be diagrams, listings, quotations, source code and more.

Anything that illustrates or supplements the text content of your web page can be a figure. With that said, most of the time figures are comprised of at least an image so that's the example we'll be using.

INSERTING A FIGURE

Remember this image from the first chapter?

Web browser figure

This is a figure.

To insert one in your web page simply wrap <figure> tags around your <img /> element.

```
<figure>
    <img src="siteraw.png" alt="SiteRaw" />
</figure>
```

Figures are almost always accompanied by captions.

In our example from the first chapter the caption reads "Web browser figure". The HTML tag for adding captions is <figcaption> and it goes inside the <figure> element, by convention after the image.

```
<figure>
    <img src="siteraw.png" alt="SiteRaw" />
    <figcaption>Web browser figure</figcaption>
</figure>
```

Earlier in this chapter I told you that images (<img />) had to be located inside paragraphs (<p>) or other block-level elements.

Well the figure tag we just discovered (<figure>) happens to be a block element, so figures can and should be located outside of paragraphs.

Here is a demonstration.

```
<p>Welcome to SiteRaw!</p>

<figure>
    <img src="siteraw.png" alt="SiteRaw" />
    <figcaption>SiteRaw is the best</figcaption>
</figure>
```

As you can see, the entire figure element is outside of the paragraph.

THE ROLE OF FIGURES

The dichotomy between inline elements and block elements is accurate but somewhat simplistic.

In reality, that's not the main reason we refrain from using figures within paragraphs... or titles inside paragraphs for that matter. Inline and block are display values. As such, they can be modified by CSS. You can turn a paragraph into an inline element and an image into a block element if you want.

Remember the golden rule of web development that I keep mentioning since the beginning of this tutorial? HTML for content, CSS for style.

The <figure> tag exists primarily for semantic purposes, the block/inline distinction being secondary.

The main reason why we don't place figures in paragraphs is that **figures are used to provide information on their own**. To supplement the paragraphs, not complete them.

If your image provides:

- no information or complementary information, put it in a paragraph.
- adjunct information, put it in a figure.

In summary, if an image is informative rather than decorative and if the information is self-contained, it should go in a figure. Don't worry too much about which case applies to your image, these aren't inflexible rules but rather proper HTML practices and valid coding conventions.

Lastly, when we introduced figures I briefly mentioned that they usually contain at least one image. They can easily hold more. Here is an example.

```
<figure>
    <img src="awesome.png" alt="SiteRaw is
awesome!" />
    <img src="amazing.png" alt="SiteRaw is
amazing!" />
    <img src="siteraw.png" alt="SiteRaw is
SiteRaw!" />

    <figcaption>What is SiteRaw?</figcaption>
</figure>
```

This case justifies the use of multiple images inside a figure as they are all related. In a moderately nonsensical fashion.

But forget that, now you know how to insert images on your website. Even better, we finished the first part of this tutorial about the HTML language.

Now we can move on to CSS.

Tired of hearing me say "we'll learn how to do X with CSS in just a moment"?

It's your lucky day! You'll finally get to learn CSS... in just a moment ;)

PART II

CSS3 DESIGN

SETTING UP CSS

Hello and wel-

My website sucks! Everything is bland... I can't add color, center my text or even place an image where I want on my page. And don't even get me started on the gross blue and purple links. I wanted to create a website not some homo pride brochure for the Roma fashion week. Isn't that the purpose of this tutorial?

Right.

Don't worry, we'll fix that very soon.

We just finished the first part of this tutorial, about the **HTML language**, and we're about to begin the second part, about the **CSS language**.

As I explained during the first chapter, you need both HTML and CSS to create a fully functional and aesthetic website.

If you want an analogy, think of HTML as the bricks that allow you to build the walls of your house and CSS as the paint that lets you brighten it up. Until now we've only worked with HTML so your house looks like... bricks.

This is the first chapter of the second part of this tutorial and it will therefore deal with the fundamentals aspects of the CSS language.

I'm sure you have more than a few interrogations.

- What is CSS?
- Why was CSS invented?
- What does CSS look like?
- Where do you write CSS code?
- Why is the author so awesome?
- Is CSS complicated?

Rest assured, we will cover everything you can imagine and more in this first chapter.

INTRODUCTION TO CSS

Having spent the first part of this course learning about HTML, we're about to dive into the CSS language that we intentionally sidelined until now.

CSS is no more complicated than HTML. It's simply a distinct language that serves a different purpose.

The CSS acronym stands for Cascading Style Sheets and as you may have guessed from the name it's used to format and stylize your website.

In HTML we learned how to tell the browser:

- I want a title here.
- I want a paragraph here.
- I want a list here.
- I want an image right after that.

With CSS we'll learn how to say:

- I want my titles to be in italic.
- I want my paragraphs in red.
- I want my lists to use a different font.
- I want my image centered.

Here is an actual example of CSS in action.

CSS IN ACTION

This demonstration will show exactly how the inclusion of the CSS language can transform a website.

Take the following HTML web page.

It's very basic and contains most of the elements we've already covered in this tutorial.

Welcome to SiteRaw

SiteRaw is the best site on the web!

Why is SiteRaw so awesome?

- Because it's awesome
- Because I'm awesome
- Because it's SiteRaw

That's why SiteRaw is **awesome** !

How to visit SiteRaw

To visit SiteRaw just go to SiteRaw.com.

Pure HTML page, no CSS

This is our rudimentary HTML page (the one you were complaining about).

Yours shouldn't look much different.

Without modifying any portion of the HTML code, let's simply add some CSS to make it easier on the eye.

Here I added some very basic CSS.

A web page with basic CSS

It's already better.

But that example is just applying the fundamentals of the CSS language. If you want to see the full potential of CSS, here's a demonstration of some advanced properties.

Advanced CSS in action

All three examples come from the exact same HTML page.

The content (HTML code) is identical but the format (CSS code) is what makes these pages look different.

 Cool! My website can finally get untarded! But how do I use CSS?

Keep reading to find out.

WRITING CSS CODE

There are three ways you can apply CSS code to a web page or a portion thereof. You can write CSS code:

- in a separate .css file (recommended)
- in the <head> tag of your page
- in the HTML tag directly by way of the style attribute

The first method is the most commonly used and you'll understand why once we've presented all three techniques.

WRITING CSS IN A SEPARATE FILE

This is the standard method of CSS inclusion and the one I

recommend.

The purpose is to place the CSS code in a `.css` file which will be included in one or more `.html` web pages. Including a CSS file in a web page is extremely easy: all you need is one HTML tag which will go in the <head> portion of your document.

Have a look at the HTML code below.

```
<!DOCTYPE html>
<html>
    <head>
        <meta charset="utf-8" />
        <title>SiteRaw</title>
        <link rel="stylesheet" href="style.
css" /> <!-- A new tag appears -->
    </head>

    <body>
        <h1>Welcome to SiteRaw</h1>

        <p>SiteRaw is the best site on the
web!</p>

        <p>Why is SiteRaw so <em>awesome</em>?
I don't even know.</p>
    </body>
</html>
```

This code looks more or less like every other HTML web page we've encountered up until now, except for the new tag in the header (on the fifth line).

This is the line I added.

```
<link rel="stylesheet" href="style.css" />
```

As you can see, this HTML tag has two attributes.

The `<link>` element indicates a relationship between the current document and an external resource. In our case the resource in question is a CSS style sheet, but it could also be an RSS feed (XML), a favicon, an iPhone or tablet icon, an internal search engine and so on.

These are the two attributes present on the `<link>` tag.

- `rel` specifies the relationship between the linked document (the CSS file) and the current document (the HTML web page). It stands for "relationship". In our case, the linked file is a style sheet so its value is `stylesheet`. Simple.
- `href` stipulates the URL of the linked resource. We already mentioned this attribute when we introduced text links in the first part of this tutorial. In our case, the value is relative path to the CSS file we want to include: `style.css`.

Now we know how to include a separate CSS file in our web page.

But I don't have a CSS file to include in my web page! I only have a `.html` web page.

That's because we haven't created our CSS file yet.

Don't worry, we'll get to that in a moment.

 Speaking of which, how do you edit CSS code? Do you need specific software?

Good question.

CSS code is created and edited in the same manner as HTML code. All you need is a text editor (Brackets, Visual Studio, Sublime, Notepad...).

Now let's create our first CSS document.

Open your text editor and create a new file. With Brackets simply go to `File > New`. Your document should be empty for now, that's not a problem. Save your file with a `.css` extension. In our example the file is called `style.css` but you can give it the name you want.

What's important is that you save your new CSS file in the same directory your current HTML web page.

Your folder should look like this.

Your HTML and CSS files

I recommend you use the same names as me for your HTML and CSS files. If you choose not to, make sure that the files names and the value of the `href` attribute match.

Here is what you should see in your text editor.

HTML and CSS text editor

Both files are currently opened in the text editor. All that's left is to see if the style sheet is properly applied to our web page. Double click on the icon of the `.html` file to open it in your browser.

You should get the following.

Welcome to SiteRaw

SiteRaw is the best site on the web!

Why is SiteRaw so *awesome*? I don't even know.

Your web page in a browser

 This sucks! It looks exactly the same as everything we've done until now!

That's because we haven't added or included any CSS yet. Remember, our CSS file is empty.

Let's remedy that.

Open your CSS document and add the following code.

```
p
{
    color: blue;
}
```

Don't worry about what this code means for the moment. Reload the web page in your browser and witness the magic of CSS.

Your paragraphs are now displayed in blue.

Welcome to SiteRaw

SiteRaw is the best site on the web!

Why is SiteRaw so *awesome*? I don't even know.

The paragraphs are blue

CSS files are not intended to be loaded directly in the browser. If you open your .css document with a web browser it will simply show your code as text. Only HTML files are interpreted by the render engine.

That is the recommended method of CSS code inclusion.

Now let's see the two others in action.

WRITING CSS IN THE HEADER

The second way of applying CSS is by writing your code inside a <style> tag within the <head> element. The following code produces exactly the same result as the demonstration above.

```
<!DOCTYPE html>
<html>
    <head>
        <meta charset="utf-8" />
        <title>SiteRaw</title>
        <style>
          p
          {
              color: blue;
          }
        </style>
    </head>

    <body>
        <h1>Welcome to SiteRaw</h1>

        <p>SiteRaw is the best site on the
web!</p>

        <p>Why is SiteRaw so <em>awesome</em>?
I don't even know.</p>
    </body>
</html>
```

Test it and see for yourself, you should get the exact same result.

WRITING CSS DIRECTLY IN A TAG

The last method is the least recommended.

Use it only for testing purposes or if you have no other alternative.

You can use the `style` attribute on the specific tag you want to format. This is a global attribute, meaning it works on any HTML element. Just write the CSS code you want to apply as the value of the `style` attribute. This example contains only the code inside the <body> element.

```
<h1>Welcome to SiteRaw</h1>

<p style="color: blue;">SiteRaw is the best
site on the web!</p>

<p>Why is SiteRaw so <em>awesome</em>? I don't
even know.</p>
```

In this case, since the CSS was applied to the first <p> element alone, only the topmost paragraph will be blue.

THE BEST METHOD OF CSS CODE INCLUSION

I don't understand why you recommend using the first method. Why do I need to create a new file for CSS? I was doing fine with just a `.html` page.

For now it may seem that separating the HTML and CSS code in two distinct files is unnecessary and only serves to makes things more complicated. In reality, far from complicating the process it's actually the most convenient solution.

Most websites are comprised of several pages that share a common CSS theme. If you were to mix HTML and CSS code in the same document, you would have to copy your CSS style from one page to another and on every page of your website. And editing it would prove nearly impossible... you would have to manually modify every page. Whereas with a separate `.css` file, all you have to do is edit the code once to modify the design of your entire website. That's why this method is the most used and the one I recommend.

APPLYING A CSS STYLE

Now we know where to write CSS code. Great.

But that's not going to be very useful unless we know how to write code in the CSS language. A bit earlier I gave you an example of CSS code without explaining it any further.

```
p
{
    color: blue;
}
```

You probably guessed its function: this code displays every paragraph in blue.

CSS code contains three essential elements:

- the **selector**: in our case we want to format the content between the <p> tags, so our selector is p. Tag names (<p>, <h1>, <strong>...) are very common selectors in CSS. Just remember to remove the angle brackets.
- the **CSS property**: the formatting effect that you want to modify. In our case it's the color of the text, so the CSS property we use is color.
- the **property value**: the value of the aforementioned CSS property. For every property you must specify a value. In our example we used the color property, so we must specify a color. In our case it was blue.

For each selector you can insert any number of properties you want.

The syntax is CSS is easy to remember.

- You enter the selector, for example a tag name without the angle brackets.
- You add braces: { and }.
- Within these braces, you can modify as many properties as you want.
- Each property starts with the property name, then a colon :, then the associated property value and finally a semi-colon ; to mark the end of the line.

Our CSS code therefore means "I want all my paragraphs to be written in blue".

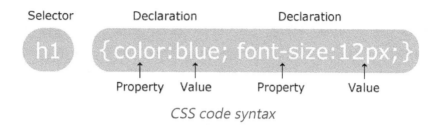
CSS code syntax

But if we change any of three elements, either the selector, the property or the value, the display effect will vary accordingly.

Let's try changing the selector.

```
h1
{
    color: blue;
}
```

Open your HTML page again and you should see the title written in blue this time. We can also change the value of the color property. Let's make our paragraphs red.

```
p
{
    color: red;
}
```

All parahraphs will now be written in red. CSS is like magic. Almost.

COMMENTS IN CSS

As with HTML, you can include comments directly in your

CSS file. Neither HTML and CSS comments are displayed or interpreted by the web browser. They are just notes and instructions about your web page or style sheet that only you can see. CSS comments are contained between two markers: /* indicates the beginning of a comment and */ indicates its end. Comments in CSS can be placed on one or several lines, as shown in the example below.

```
/*

This is my CSS style sheet.

It turns every paragraph red!

*/

p
{
    color: red; /* Paragraphs will be red. */
}
```

CSS comments aren't used very often but you should know how they work in case you ever need to document your code.

ADVANCED CSS SELECTORS

Let's talk a bit about selectors.

In this chapter, we learned how to use CSS to tell the browser:

- I want my titles <h1> written in blue.
- I want my paragraphs <p> written in red.

But what about other commands?

What if we want to say:

- I want my titles <h1> and my paragraphs <p> written in pink.
- I want only the first paragraph <p> written in blue.
- I want every emphasis <em> within a title <h1> written in red.
- I want every paragraph <p> that directly follows a title <h1> written in green.

Those are some inappropriately specific directions. But can CSS execute them?

Of course it can.

APPLYING A STYLE TO MULTIPLE TAGS

Imagine that we want both our title <h1> and our emphasized text <em> to be pink.

You could very well use the following code.

```
h1
{
    color: deeppink;
}


em
{
    color: deeppink;
}
```

Don't worry about deeppink, it's just a different shade of pink. Try it out and see if everything works.

It works... but isn't it kind of repetitive to write every tag you need to format? What if I want three or four tags to be blue, do I need to write the same code three or four times?

As it turns out you don't need to repeat any portion of your code. In the same way you can add multiple CSS properties to a single HTML tag (for example color and font-size), you can also use multiple HTML tags as the CSS selector.

To combine two CSS selectors just separate them by a coma.

```
h1, em { color: red; }
```

This code produces the exact same results as the longer version shown higher above.

134

You may have noticed that I shortened the CSS code slightly on my last demonstration. Specifically, I wrote every element (selector, property and value) on the same line. It's entirely optional. For this tutorial, I'll continue to use the longer code structure as it is more readable.

You can format as many tags one after the other as you want.

THE CLASS AND ID ATTRIBUTES

Everything we've seen so far still falls short on one aspect.

If you tell the browser to render your paragraphs in blue, than every occurrence of the <p> element will be displayed in blue.

What if you want separate paragraphs to be formatted differently? What if you only want the first paragraph to be pink?

That's a good question. You could always use the style attribute to apply CSS only to the specified tag but we've already advised against this method.

Fortunately there is a simple way to solve this problem.

We can use one of two attributes:

- the class attribute
- the id attribute

These are called global attributes as they work on every HTML element (style is also a global attribute). Perhaps you remember the id attribute from chapter on links when we used it to create anchors. You gave it whichever value you wanted and that value served as an identifier for the HTML tag. The only requirement was that no two tags could share the same id.

The class attribute works in a similar fashion. The difference is that you can have as many elements share a class as you want. Here is the example of a paragraph belonging to the "siteraw" class.

```
<p class="siteraw">SiteRaw is the best site on
the web!</p>
```

Since we are using a class attribute we can apply it to several HTML elements.

```
<h1>Welcome to SiteRaw</h1>

<p class="siteraw">SiteRaw is the best site on
the web!</p>

<p>Why is SiteRaw so <em class="siteraw">awesome</
em>? I don't even know.</p>
```

Both the first paragraph (<p>) and the emphasis (<em>) belong to the class siteraw. We can use this attribute in CSS to say: I only want the tags marked "siteraw" to be written in orange.

To select a class attribute in CSS, simply enter its name preceded by a dot . as the selector.

```
.siteraw
{
    color: orangered;
}
```

Try it out. Only your first paragraph and the emphasis will have a different color.

The id attribute is used in the exact same way as class. The only difference is that it is prefixed by a hash character (#) rather than a dot (.) in the CSS style sheet.

Here is an HTML demonstration code.

```
<h1 id="siteraw">Welcome to SiteRaw</h1>
```

And the associated CSS.

```
#siteraw
{
    color: blue;
}
```

Other than that, id works exactly in the same way as the class attribute.

GENERAL PURPOSE TAGS

Let's say you want to apply a specific format to some words that were not originally surrounded by tags. For instance, let's have a look at the first paragraph in our demo.

```
<p>SiteRaw is the best site on the web!</p>
```

What if we want to have the text "SiteRaw" displayed in red?

The problem with class and id is that they are attributes and as such must be used on an specific HTML tag. But there is no tag that surrounds the word "SiteRaw" alone.

We could always insert a <em> or <strong> tag, add some color and remove the inherent text effects (italic or bold respectively). But remember the rule of web development? HTML is for content, CSS is for style. To add a <em> or <strong> element would imply that the text contained in these tags requires emphasis. What is we just need to format it without emphasizing it?

Luckily, there are two tags in the HTML language that permit exactly that: they are called general purpose tags.

These tags share the particularity that they don't communicate any semantic information to the user agent. But that doesn't mean that they are useless, quite the contrary. You can think of them as placeholder elements and are used mostly for CSS formatting.

These are the two general purpose tags that exist in HTML.

- <span> is an inline element like <em> and <strong>. Inline elements take only as much width as required and don't start on a new line. They are usually employed within a block element. This is the tag we'll use for our example.
- <div> is a block element like <p> and <h1>. It stands for "division". Block-level tags occupy the entire horizontal space of their parent container thereby forcing a new line break before and after the element.

We've already mentioned the block and inline dichotomy so you're probably familiar with it by now. For our example, we only want the text "SiteRaw" to be affected by CSS so we will use the <span> tag.

```
<p><span class="siteraw">SiteRaw</span> is the
best site on the web!</p>
```

And the CSS code.

```
.siteraw
{
    color: red;
}
```

This should color any element with the class value "SiteRaw" - in our case only the first word - in red.

Since we are only applying a style to a single tag we could use either class or id for this purpose, it would make no difference. If we needed to select two separate portions of text however, we would have to use class.

MORE ADVANCED SELECTORS

You now know how to apply a CSS style to either a single tag, multiple tags or specific tags marked by either the class or id attributes. Here are some other ways to target specific portion of your content using CSS.

THE UNIVERSAL SELECTOR

What if you want to target every tag in your HTML document? Simply use the universal selector *.

```
* { color: red; }
```

This selector isn't used very often as most HTML tags inherit CSS properties from their parent elements. You might have noticed that when we turned our paragraphs blue, the <em> tag contained within a paragraph was also displayed in blue.

We didn't need to stipulate that we wanted both <p> and <em> elements to be blue because <em> inherited the color property from its parent element (<p>). As you, if you wanted to make every occurrence of text on your web page to be red, you would modify the color property on either the <body> or the <html> tags rather than use the universal selector.

This selector still has its occasional uses and you should at least know it exists in case you ever need it.

A TAG WITHIN ANOTHER

Take this HTML code.

```
<h3>Welcome to <em>SiteRaw</em>!</h3>
```

What if we want to select the <em> inside the <h3> element?

Technically we could add a class or id attribute to the emphasis and apply our style to that instead, but isn't there an easier way? Let's find out.

```
h3 em { color: red; }
```

This code selects every <em> tag inside an <h3> element.

The syntax is A B, not to be confused with A, B which selects both the A and B elements regardless of their containers. This is called a **descendant selector** or **child selector**.

DIRECT CHILD SELECTOR

Sometimes the descendant selector goes a bit overboard and formats more than we want. The reason is that it selects every occurrence of tag A contained in HTML element B.

To understand a bit better, look at the following code.

```
<p>
    <span>Why is <span>SiteRaw</span> so
awesome?</span>
</p>
```

Let's try to format our code using the selector we just learned about.

```
span { color: blue; }

p span { color: red; }
```

This tells the browser: I want every <span> to be blue but every <span> within a <p> to be red. The second style overrides the first and indeed, our text is now red. Try it.

 But wait... Why is the text "SiteRaw" red? Shouldn't it be blue since it's not contained within a <p>?

That's not exactly true.

The "SiteRaw" text is contained within a <span>, which is itself inside a <span>... inside a <p>. The nesting hierarchy is as follows: p > span > span. So technically, it is contained within a <p> which is why the text is red. But I see your point. What if we want to only select the tags that are direct children of a parent element? In our example that would mean only formatting those whose hierarchy is p > span and leaving out the "SiteRaw" text.

For that we have the **direct child selector**. Let's update our CSS code.

```
span { color: blue; }
p > span { color: red; }
```

The "SiteRaw" text is not affected by the second line of our CSS so its formatting reverts to the original rule (first line) that applies to all <span> tags: blue text.

The syntax of a direct child selector is A > B. It selects every instance of a B element of which the direct parent is an A tag.

A TAG AFTER ANOTHER

Let's go back to our demo page.

```
<h1>Welcome to SiteRaw</h1>

<p>SiteRaw is the best site on the web!</p>

<p>Why is SiteRaw so <em>awesome</em>? I don't
even know.</p>
```

Throughout this chapter, we saw how we could format the the paragraph only by assigning it a class or id attribute. But is that the only way? What if we want to select every paragraph that immediately follows an <h1> title? Try this out.

```
h1 + p { color: red; }
```

This code selects the first <p> tag located after an <h1> title. The syntax is A + B so don't confuse it with what we just learned above.

This is called the **adjacent sibling selector**.

GENERAL SIBLING SELECTOR

Let's see the HTML code first and the explanations second.

```
<p>Blue</p>

<div>
    <p>Blue</p>

    <h3>Welcome to SiteRaw</h3>

    <p>RED</p> <!-- This tag -->

    <div>
        <p>Blue</p>
    </div>

    <div>
        <h3>Guess the color</h3>
        <p>RED</p> <!-- This tag -->
    </div>

    <p>RED</p> <!-- And this tag -->
</div>

<p>Blue</p>
```

This code seems pretty self explanatory.

You have to format every tag that says "RED" without modifying the HTML code. And before you ask, there is no selector that allows you to mark an element based on the text it contains.

The answer only takes one line of CSS code.

```
h3 ~ p { color: red; }
```

We should also make the default text blue but I trust you know how to do that by now. So what is this new selector? It's called the **general sibling selector** and combines a few properties from the selectors we've learned about previously.

The A ~ B selector marks all instances of B elements that follow and share the same parent as an A tag. In our example it means that the <p> tag must:

- share the same parent as a <h3> tag
- come after a <h3> title (though not necessarily directly after)

Try it out. The three tags that say "RED" will be displayed in red. Success.

A TAG WITH AN ATTRIBUTE

Can CSS select a tag that holds a specific attributes? Let's find out.

```
a[title] { color: red; }
```

This will affect every <a> tag that has a title attribute regardless of its value. What if you want to specify a value?

```
a[title="SiteRaw"] { color: red; }
```

This will only affect <a> elements whose title attribute has the value SiteRaw.

It will not format:

- tags other than <a> (regardless of attributes)
- tags with no title attribute
- tags whose title attribute's value isn't SiteRaw

And finally, what if you want it to contain the value SiteRaw rather than check for exact match?

```
a[title*="SiteRaw"] { color: red; }
```

The only change is the addition of an asterisk *.

COMBO SELECTORS

Lastly, know that you can combine multiple CSS selectors into one mega-selector. For example you can merge the type selector with the class selector.

```css
p.siteraw { color: orangered; }

em#siteraw { color: orangered; }
```

This code will format every <p> element of the "siteraw" class and every <em> element of the "siteraw" id. Here is a demonstration.

```html
<p id="siteraw">Welcome to <em
id="siteraw">SiteRaw</em>.</p>

<p>Welcome to <em class="siteraw">SiteRaw</
em>.</p>

<p class="siteraw">Welcome to <em>SiteRaw</
em>.</p>
```

Try it out. Only the first emphasis and last paragraph should be orange.

 *When we write .siteraw or #siteraw alone as the selector, what we're implying is that we want *.siteraw or *#siteraw meaning any tag that possesses that class or id. Both methods produce the same result. The shorter form is generally preferred so it's the one we'll be using in this tutorial.*

Summary

There are a few more cases we haven't covered, not least of which what we call pseudo-classes. They almost deserve a chapter of their own. We'll get to them soon enough.

You don't have to remember every single selector of the CSS language. Most of the examples presented in this chapter are of situational use only. I can't remember the last time, if there even was one, where I needed to format links that contained a title attribute differently from the rest of the links. The three main selectors you should remember are as follows.

Example	Selector	Explanation
h1	Type Selector	Selects an element by its tag name (type).
.class	Class Selector	Selects an element by its class attribute value.
#id	ID Selector	Selects an element by its id attribute value.

These are the principal CSS selectors we will be using in this tutorial.

TEXT FORMATTING

R eady to start designing your website like a true web developer? Look no further, this chapter is for you. In the last chapter we learned the basics of the CSS language: what it is, why it's used, where to write CSS code and how to apply a CSS style to a specific HTML element. Text formatting simply means that we're going to modify the appearance of text content.

 About that... I don't want to complain but we only ever learned how to change the color of our text. Is that all there is to CSS?

It's true that we have only seen one CSS property until now. But that was just for demonstration purposes so you could see the changes in real time on your web page. From now on, we'll be using many more CSS properties to format our text.

In this chapter we'll learn how to adjust the text size, modify the font, apply a text effect such as italics, align the paragraphs.

At the end of this chapter your website will (finally) start to look like something.

TEXT SIZE

To change the size of your text, all you need is one CSS property: font-size. But what do we enter for its value?

There are two methods for stipulating text size in CSS:

- an **absolute value** specifies a font size in pixels, inches, points, millimeters and so on.
- a **relative value** specifies a font size as a percentage of the default text size of the page.

Both methods are used significantly for web designing.

AN ABSOLUTE SIZE

To define an absolute size in CSS we use what is called length values. These can be points, pixels, inches, centimeters, millimeters or even pica. For web development, the preferred format is almost always the pixel.

Other length values such as inches are less suited for screen display.

Here is how you use pixels with the `font-size` property.

```
p { font-size: 16px; }
```

The length unit here is the pixel so we append its symbol px to the value we want. The text in your paragraphs should now be 16 pixels high... which should not change anything as 16 pixels is the default font size on most browsers. Try using a larger or smaller size to see the text change on your web page.

 As I've mentioned, px is the symbol for the pixel unit. There are other absolute units such as the inch in, the centimeter cm or the point pt. Pixel lengths are generally preferred for web usage.

A RELATIVE SIZE

Relative font sizes are, as their name suggests, relative.

 Ok. That's great. But what does it means? I thought we already had pixels, inches and everything else?

Pixels and other units are absolute values.

That means 1 pixel will always measure 1 pixel.

Relative values on the other hand use a different set of units that are flexible, adaptable and most importantly context depended. The context usually being the browser's default settings, or those of your web page if you've decided to overwrite them. One way of specifying a relative value is by downright entering their sizes.

Here is a list of the different values you can set and their meaning.

- `xx-small` : extremely small
- `x-small` : very small
- `small` : small
- `medium` : medium
- `large` : large
- `x-large` : very large
- `xx-large` : maternal filiation comedy

You can use these values in your CSS code as follows.

```
h1 { font-size: large; }

p { font-size: small; }
```

While this method works, there is an obvious drawback: there are only seven sizes available. Fortunately you can also use other units to define a relative font size.

One of those is the em unit.

In CSS, one em is equal to the font size of the parent element.

- If you want a regular text size, stick with 1.
- I you want a larger text size, enter a value greater than 1 such as 1.5em.
- I you want a smaller text size, enter a value lower than 1 such as 0.8em.

Decimals are of course preferred as 2em would double the size of the text.

Here is how you use this unit in CSS.

```
h1 { font-size: 1.5em; }

p { font-size: 0.8em; }
```

There are other units available. You can use em, rem, ex or percentages %. Besides rem which is a variation of em, they all have different bases.

 Ok. That's great. But what does it means? I thought we already had pixels, inches and everything else?

You don't.

That's the point of relative values: their absolute values are conditioned on either the format of a parent element or the settings of the browser. By default, 1em is worth 16px for most desktop browser. But that value may be lower on certain smartphones and tablets. Additionally, the em unit is dependent on the size of parent or ancestor elements.

For example take this HTML code.

```
<div>
    <p>Welcome to <span>SiteRaw</span></p>
</div>
```

As we said, the default value of 1em on most browsers is 16px. But if the parent element has a larger font size it will affect the base value of the em unit.

```
div { font-size: 20px; }

p { font-size: 1em; }

span { font-size: 1.5em; }
```

Within the <div> element the value of 1em is not longer 16px but 20px. And any text within a <span> tag will have a font size of 30px.

 If you want the relative values of em without them being affected by parent or ancestor elements, you can use the rem unit. It's identical to em but it ignores parent tags and only depends on the font size of the root element, the <html> tag.

FONT FAMILY

In CSS, the font family is the typeface that will be applied to your text. Usually they are simply called "fonts" but the names aren't necessarily interchangeable. Regardless of semantics and terminology, applying a font (or a typeface) to a portion of text on your web page is very easy. The only issue that comes up is the availability of the font. For a font to be displayed correctly we need the user to have that font installed. Otherwise, if a user doesn't have the font you want to render on your page, the browser will apply a default typeface that may have little visual similarities with what you were expecting.

Granted, everyone has "Arial" installed... But what about the newest "SEWER2154.otf" font that you were planning to use on your edgy extreme metal website? The good news is that since CSS3 you can embed a font directly from your style sheet. I'll explain how to do so in a moment.

MODIFYING THE FONT

As I said, changing the font is easy.

The CSS property that allows you to specify a typeface is font-family.

Here is how it's used.

```
font-family: font;
```

Just replace the value `font` with whatever typeface identifier or font family names you want to use. We'll see which fonts are most appropriate for web usage in just a second. The `font-family` property also allows you to indicate several font names, separated by commas.

```
font-family: font1, font2, font3, font4;
```

Every font name after the first one is an alternative font. The reason for supplying a prioritized list rather than a single font is that the other fonts will act as a back-up in case the user doesn't have the first font installed. In our example, the browser will first check to see if the user has `font1` installed. If he has, everything goes well and it is displayed. If he doesn't, the browser proceeds to check with `font2` and so on all the way to `font4`. The last font is a fallback font or last resort font that everyone is sure to have. It's usually `serif` or `sans-serif`.

 Ok, but what fonts can I use on the web? You still haven't given us a list of font names!

Technically you can use any font you want.

If a font exists, it can be displayed on the web.

The problem is with operating system and browser compatibility. Luckily, there are a few generic fonts also called web safe fonts that are deemed reasonably likely to be present on most if not all computers.

WEB SAFE FONTS

Web safe fonts are the fonts that ensure maximum compatibility with most browsers and operating systems.

Here is a list of the most common web safe fonts:

- Arial
- **Arial Black**
- Comic Sans MS
- Courier New
- Georgia
- **Helvetica**
- **Impact**
- Palatino
- Times New Roman
- Trebuchet MS
- Verdana

Many web developers recommend specifying at least three or four fonts, starting with the font you want and ending with either `serif` or `sans-serif`. I find it a bit excessive but it's really up to you and how many alternatives you want to offer.

 You keep talking about `serif` and `sans-serif`, what are they?

In this context they are fonts. They're the most basic ones you can find and they will always be rendered even if for whatever reason the user has no fonts installed on his computer. But serif and sans serif have a wider meaning that predates web development. In typography, serifs are semi-structural elements added for embellishment to the characters of a typeface. As such all fonts can be divided based on whether their letters possess serifs or not. In the latter case they're called sans serif fonts.

Serif and sans serif

Serif fonts are considered easier to read in printed as the letters are more distinctive. Most books are usually published with a serif typeface. Times New Roman and Georgia are serif fonts whereas Arial and Verdana are sans serif.

This distinction is somewhat important when indicating alternative fonts. Your fallback fonts should if possible be of the same type as the preferred font. For example, if I'm aiming for a sans serif font my CSS code would be the following.

```
p { font-family: Impact, "Arial Black", Arial,
Verdana, sans-serif; }
```

All the possible fonts are sans-serif.

If the font name includes spaces I suggest you surround it with quotes as I've done with "Arial Black". It becomes necessary when the font name contains numbers or special characters.

In addition to serif and sans serif, there are other font types such as monospace, cursive and fantasy. They aren't used much and the difference in style is minimal compared to serif/ sans serif.

USING A CUSTOM FONT

You now know how to change the typeface of your text and provide alternative fonts to the user.

 These fonts suck. I want to use my own fonts instead of Arial and Verdana.

For a long time this wasn't possible. You either had to use a web safe font or try and guess which fonts were installed on the user's computer and hope you were right.

Then CSS3 came around and it's now possible to embed any font directly in your CSS style sheet.I'll be the first one to admit that it's a pretty cool feature but there are still quite a few drawbacks to this practice.

These are some of the few inconveniences of this method.

- Embedding a font means that the user will have to load it through his browser. Some fonts may weigh up to 1 MB or more and that means he'll reach puberty before he finishes loading your website.
- Many fonts are subject to copyright, making them illegal for use on your website. There are still many free alternatives so this isn't much of a problem if you know the license of your font.
- There are several font formats and not every format is compatible with every browser. This is less of a problem

today as we'll see further on, but it can complicate things for those using outdated browsers.

The last two points aren't as big of a deal as they once were. The biggest impediment to using custom fonts is the size of each file, so if you do use them make sure it's with parsimony. But since we started talking about font formats, let's take a quick detour and introduce them properly.

THE DIFFERENT FONT FORMATS

Just as image files have different formats depending among other factors on their method of compression, font files also have distinct formats that affect the way their data is stored.

Here is a list of the main font formats used on the web.

- `.ttf` : TrueType Font. Works with Internet Explorer 9 and onward and all other browsers.
- `.eot` : Embedded OpenType. Works with Internet Explorer only, on all versions. This is a proprietary format produced by Microsoft.
- `.otf` : OpenType Font. Similar to .ttf, works on all browsers except the older versions of Internet Explorer (prior to IE 9).
- `.svg` : Scalable Vector Graphics. For a long time this was the only format supported on iPhone and iPad browsers. Works on most versions of Safari.
- `.woff` : Web Open Font Format. A newer format

163

designed specifically for the web. Works on all recent browsers.

Generally, you want to stick with `.ttf`, `.otf` and `.woff`.

Some web developers prefer to provide a font version in every format to ensure maximum compatibility.

	EOT	OTF / TTF	WOFF	WOFF2	SVG
IE 8-11	X				
IE 9-11	X	X	X		
Edge 12 - 14		X	X		
Firefox 40-45		X	X	X	
Chrome 43-49		X	X	X	
Safari 8-9		X	X		X
Opera 32-35		X	X	X	
iOS Safari 8.4-9.3		X	X		X
Android 4.4 - 66		X	X		
Chrome for Android 66		X	X	X	

Font formats and browser compatibility

DECLARING A NEW FONT

To define a custom font you first need a font file in one of the aforementioned formats. There are many websites on the Internet that propose free fonts to download. One font directory I can recommend is Font Squirrel, but there are many others you can try out.

Once you've downloaded your font files, extract them to the same directory as your CSS style sheet.

This is what you should have in your file explorer.

Fonts files next to the style sheet

In this demonstration the two fonts files are `Learning.otf` and `Rust.otf`.

Using a custom font in CSS is a twofold process. First you have to declare a new font and then apply it on the selector on you want. We already know how do perform the second action so let's focus on the declaration first.

This is how you declare a new font in CSS.

```css
@font-face {
    font-family: 'SiteRaw';
    src: url('SiteRaw.otf');
}
```

The syntax looks similar to that of a selector but it's actually something completely different.

Anything started with a commercial at @ in CSS is called a "rule" or "at-rule".

By convention, these go at the top of your CSS document before any style formatting. This rule is named `@font-face` and contains two "properties". I use quotes because while they look like CSS properties, they are in fact called descriptors and work in a slightly different fashion.

Here of the two descriptors we used.

- `font-family` declares the name of the font. In our example it's `SiteRaw` but it can be anything you want. It's simply the identifier that we'll write when we want to apply the font.
- `src` declares the source (location) of the font file. In our example it's `SiteRaw.otf`. But if I wanted to use one of the two fonts files from the image above, I would write either `Rust.otf` or `Learning.otf`.

This short code just "created" a new font with the name `SiteRaw` and whose file was located at `SiteRaw.otf` in the same directory as our CSS style sheet.

 But what if I have several font formats for the same font?

Easy. Just enter as many formats as you want. The browser will automatically download the one it can read and ignore the rest.

```
@font-face {
    font-family: 'SiteRaw';
    src: url('SiteRaw.eot') format('eot'),
         url('SiteRaw.woff') format('woff'),
         url('SiteRaw.ttf') format('truetype'),
         url('SiteRaw.svg') format('svg');
}
```

Now that we know how to declare a new font, all that's left to learn is how to apply it to a specific HTML element. This is perhaps the easiest part... all you need to do is use the `font-family` property. But instead of using a generic font name you simply enter the name of the font you previously declared. Just make sure the custom font name you used in the `@font-face` matches the one you use in your selector properties.

The following example will show you how to define and apply two custom fonts in CSS.
First the HTML code.

```
<h1>Welcome to SiteRaw</h1>

<p>SiteRaw is the best site on the web.</p>
```

Nothing special here.

Now let's move on to the CSS code.

```
@font-face {
    font-family: 'Rust';
    src: url('Rust.otf');
}

@font-face {
    font-family: 'Learning';
    src: url('Learning.otf');
}

h1 { font-family: 'Rust'; }

p { font-family: 'Learning'; }
```

We defined two custom fonts and applied them respectively to the <h1> and <p> elements.

Here is what you should see in your browser.

WELCOME TO SITERAW

SiteRaw is the best site on the web.

Custom fonts with CSS

Results obviously depend on which fonts you have chosen.

TYPOGRAPHICAL DECORATIONS

CSS has many properties that allow you to stylize your text.

You can apply italics, bold, underline, overline and even make your text blink. Just don't actually use the last one, blinking text is a serious PTSD trigger for veteran web developers.

 Why do I need CSS for that? I thought we already had the <em> tag for italic text!

Where did you learn that? Certainly not from me.

In fact, during the Organize your text chapter I specifically stated that HTML highlight tags such as <strong>, <em> and <mark> were not to be used for text formatting. *HTML for content, CSS for style.* Repeat that every day if you have to.

HTML tags such as <em> and <strong> are used to emphasize words. They communicate to the browsing agent that their content is to be treated as important text. By default, most browsers will apply a certain text style depending on the tag (bold for <strong>, italics for <em> and so on). But that is not the purpose of these elements. Applying bold, italics, underlined and other text decorations belongs to the realm of CSS.

Let's learn how to do it.

ITALICS IN CSS

With CSS you can apply italics to any HTML element you choose, be they paragraphs, titles or anything else. To apply italics in CSS you use `font-style`.

This property can take three values:

- `italic` : the text will be written in italics.
- `oblique` : the text will be displayed obliquely.
- `normal` : the text will be set back to normal (default).

Here is a demonstration.

```
p { font-style: italic; }
```

This code will make make your paragraphs italic. But let's say you want to remove the italics from the <em> tag.

```
em { font-style: normal; }
```

With this, the <em> element will no longer be italicized.

 What is the difference between italic and oblique text? They both look the same to me.

An oblique is a roman font that has been skewed a certain number of degrees, usually between eight and twelve.

An italic on the other hand is a variation of the character set that comprises the font, often times with additional calligraphy used to accentuate the slant. Italics are an angled typeface with a distinct character set from its roman equivalent. Obliques are just a geometrical transformation of the original font.

Italic vs oblique text

For italics to be displayed properly the user must have the italic version of the font installed. If he doesn't, the text is simply skewered and an oblique effect is created on the fly.

As for which effect is best, the italic version is usually preferred by web developers but that's just convention.

BOLD IN CSS

Let's move on to the bold text effect.

Once again, the proper why to apply bold formatting is not through the HTML element <strong>. The CSS property for bold text is font-weight.

There are quite a few values this property can take so let's start with the two main ones.

- bold : the text will be displayed in bold.
- normal : the text will be displayed normally (default).

Here is an example on how to make your paragraphs bold.

```
p { font-weight: bold; }
```

Nothing too complicated here.

CSS bold text

 What about the other values? You said those two were just the main ones.

In addition to `bold` and `normal` you can also use `bolder` and `lighter` which are respectively bolder and lighter than the inherited font weight. There is also a third way of indicating a font weight, through numerical values.

- `100` : Lightest.
- `200` : Bolder than 100, lighter than 300.
- `300` : Bolder than 200, lighter than 400.
- `400` : Bolder than 300, lighter than 500. Normal.
- `500` : Bolder than 400, lighter than 600.
- `600` : Bolder than 500, lighter than 700.
- `700` : Bolder than 600, lighter than 800. Bold.
- `800` : Bolder than 700, lighter than 900.
- `900` : Boldest.

While this method offers more options than the first one, these nine numerical values shouldn't be relied upon to apply a font weight consistently. Many fonts contain fewer than nine bold variants, so unless you tested the font first I recommend you stick with bold and normal.

CSS font weight example

UNDERLINE IN CSS

What about applying underline and other text styles? The CSS property for this is aptly named `text-decoration`.

It can take the following values.

- `underline` : underlined.
- `line-through` : struck through.
- `overline` : a line above.
- `blink` : blinking text. Seriously, don't use it. It doesn't even work on most browsers anymore.
- `none` : normal (default).

The following CSS code will add an underline effect to the <h1> element and remove the default underline from any links on your web page.

```
h1 { text-decoration: underline; }

a { text-decoration: none; }
```

You can apply multiple values by separating them with spaces.

```
p { text-decoration: overline underline; }

p { text-decoration: overline underline line-through; }
```

Try it out and see the result for yourself.

 I want to change the color of the underline. How can I do that?

Quite easily. You can use the property `text-decoration-color`. For its value just specify any color you want. By default it will be the same color as your text.

```
p {
    text-decoration: underline;
    text-decoration-color: red;
}
```

The above code will underline every paragraph in red without changing the color of the text.

ALIGNMENT AND FLOATS

There are two ways you can handle alignment in CSS.

You can either adjust the way the text is aligned within a block element, or you can modify the way the block element itself is aligned by having it float either to the left or to the right.

HTML FOR CONTENT, CSS FOR STYLE

CSS allows you to specify the way inline text is aligned within a block element. Your text can be aligned either to the left, to the right, to the center or even configured to take up all the horizontal space available. The CSS property used to define typographical alignments is unsurprisingly called text-align.

Here are the values it can take.

- left : the text will be left-aligned (default).
- center : the text will be centered.
- right : the text will be right-aligned.
- justify : the text will be justified.

Justified content simply means that the text any white space at the ends of lines. Most books and other printed media have justified text.

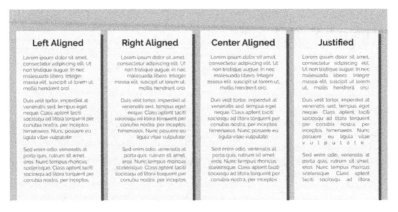

Alignment types

Let's see the different alignments in action.

```
h1 { text-align: center; }

p { text-align: justify; }

.footer { text-align: right; }
```

The result is shown below.

Welcome to SiteRaw

SiteRaw is the best site on the web. SiteRaw is the best site on the web. *Don't believe me?* SiteRaw is the best site on the web.

Proof: Seriously, it is.

The different CSS alignments

You can't change the alignment of an inline element such as <span>, <em> or <a>. It must be used on either a paragraph <p>, a title <h1> or any other block element.

FLOATING ITEMS IN CSS

177

There is another method of alignment in CSS called the **float**, commonly and more appropriately called text wrap. Floats work in a different way than typographical alignment. Whereas text alignments format only the content inside of a block element, floats affect the entire element. The following image should give you an idea of how they're used on a web page.

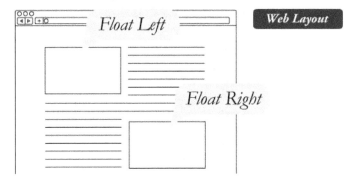

Floating elements in CSS

As you can see, the image is floating to the right. The CSS property you need to modify the float of an element is called... float. Who would have thought?

Here are the values it can take:

- none : there is no float (default).
- left : the element will float on the left.
- right : the element will float on the right.

In theory, the float property can only be applied to a block-level element.

But that's not a problem since inline elements with a float will automatically be converted to a block layout. You can therefore use float on any HTML tag you want: an image, a title, a paragraph and so on. With that said, floats work best when the affected element has a defined width.

For our example we'll use an image.

A FLOATING IMAGE

To apply a float to an image, or any HTML element, you first need the appropriate HTML code. Here is what we'll use in our example.

```
<p><img src="siteraw.png" alt="Welcome to
SiteRaw" /></p>

<p>Welcome to SiteRaw. SiteRaw is the best site
on the web. Why is SiteRaw so awesome? And why
do all your demos contain the same text?</p>

<p>Who knows...</p>
```

 A common mistake is to place the floating element after the text. Whether you want it to float to the right or to the left, it must be above the text that surrounds it.

For now there is no CSS code, so you won't notice anything different. Let's type the following in our CSS file.

```
img
{
        float: left;
}
```

And... that's it. Just one property. This code will make every <img /> tag float to the left. If you want it to float to the right instead, just replace the value of the float property accordingly.

CLEARING A FLOAT

When you insert a floating element, the text naturally wraps around it to one side or the other. But what if you want some of your text to be underneath the floating element? As you can see, in our example we have two paragraphs. How can we make the second one not be affected by the image's float?

CSS has a property that allows you to do just that. Elements affected by the clear property will automatically disregard any floating element and be moved down (cleared) below it.

Here are the values it can take.

- left : the element is moved down after a left float
- right : the element is moved down after a right float
- both : the element is moved down after any float

In practice we'll be using mostly the third option.

Let's apply it to our demonstration. First, the HTML code.

```
<p><img src="siteraw.png" alt="Welcome to
SiteRaw" /></p>

<p>Welcome to SiteRaw. SiteRaw is the best site
on the web. Why is SiteRaw so awesome? And why
do all your demos contain the same text?</p>

<p class="siteraw">Who knows...</p>
```

Nothing very different from what we saw earlier, the only addition being the class identifier applied to the second paragraph.

Now for the CSS code.

```
img { float: left; }

.siteraw { clear: both; }
```

That's it. The second paragraph should now start below the floating image as shown in the following figure.

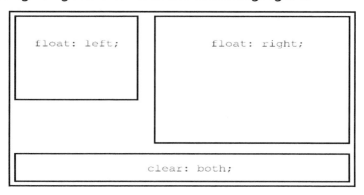

Float and clear in action

You now know both methods to align elements in CSS.

COLOR AND BACKGROUND

L et's continue our guide of the essential CSS properties. In this chapter we are mainly going to talk about the properties related to colors and backgrounds. Yes, plural. As you will see, there are many different ways to adjust the color of an element in CSS. In addition to that we're also going to cover how to change the color of the background, create gradients, adjust transparency and more. CSS is not done impressing you.

TEXT COLOR

Since we have to start somewhere, let's begin with the concept of colors. We briefly saw the CSS property `color` in the first chapter of this second part, Setting up CSS.

It's usage is quite intuitive, you simply indicate the name of the color you want to apply as a value.

```
p { color: red; }
```

This code will turn all your paragraphs red. But that's far from the only way you can use the `color` property. We'll have a look at the different ways of specifying a color, there are many.

Colors in CSS

COLORS BY NAME

One easy and convenient way to specify a color is simply by entering its name or keyword. For example.

```
h1 { color: magenta; }
```

```
p { color: olive; }
```

```
strong { color: red; }
```

This code is rather self-explanatory, it turns your titles magenta, your paragraphs olive (a yellowish shade of green) and your emphasizes red.

That's the method we've used until now but it comes with its drawbacks: a limited number of colors to choose from. It's fine as long as we're working with a rudimentary pallet of colors, but it's not doing CSS justice to restrict our choices to only the colors which dispose of a name.

What if we want a shade of red somewhere between Crimson and FireBrick? Luckily, there are other methods we can use to indicate a color with more accuracy.

COLORS BY HEXADECIMAL

Most monitors can display over 16 million colors and CSS allows you to use any tone you want on your web page. Obviously, for practical reasons, not every shade of red has an established name. We need another way of specifying the color we want. One of such ways is the **hexadecimal notation**. This is the most commonly used format for indicating colors on the web. Here is a demonstration of this nomenclature.

```
h1 { color: #FF0000; }
```

This code will make your titles red.

I don't get it! Wouldn't it be easier to just write "red" like we used to do?

That remark is true for this example, but hexadecimal enables you to specify colors in a much less restrictive way than by typing their names. If you've never seen hexadecimal employed before, it's just a different numeral system from what you're used to (decimal). The numbers are exactly the same as decimals, but instead of having digits go from 0 to 9 (decimal) they go from 0 to 15 (hexadecimal).

 You've probably heard of at least one other numeral system before: binary, which goes from 0 to 1.

The base (or radix, for mathematicians) is therefore 16 instead of 10. Since we don't have symbols for digits higher than 9, we had to borrow them from our Latin alphabet. The numbers "ten" to "fifteen" become single-digit numbers represented by A to F ("ten" is A, "eleven" is B... "fifteen" is F).

The hexadecimal notation is sometimes and more accurately called **hex triplet** as it consists of three distinct sections. In total you have 2563 = 166 = 224 = 16,777,216 colors to choose from.

The number in our example is #FF0000.

Hex triplets always start with a hash character (#) in CSS and most other computing applications. After that we have six characters from the hexadecimal numeral system. They work by pairs and, from left to right, indicate the quantities of red, green and blue, also called the RGB (Red-Green-Blue) value of our color in the following way.

- Red: 00 (no red) to FF (max red)
- Green: 00 (no green) to FF (max green)
- Blue: 00 (no blue) to FF (max blue)

As you will have guessed, #000000 (no color) is black and #FFFFFF (max of everything) is white.

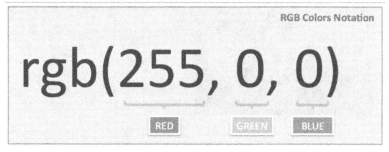

The hexadecimal color notation

The color we used in our example was #FF0000. Maximum red, no green, no blue. The final result is obviously red.

But what if I want a light blue color, something halfway between navy blue and cyan? From the top of my head I could try #00BAFF. No red, about 75% of green and maximum blue.

Here is the result as shown in Photoshop.

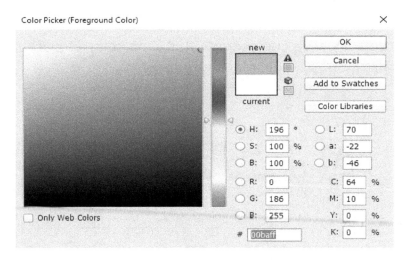

Photoshop hexadecimal color wheel

Drawing software programs like Photoshop are convenient in that they allow you to pick the color you want directly from a color wheel and simply copy and paste the result in your CSS file. If you don't have such software you can also try Adobe's Color Picker directly from their website (color.adobe.com).

I used uppercase letters in my hexadecimal colors simply because they are easier to distinguish than lowercase ones. You can use whichever form you want, there are no rules or conventions. #FFFFFF is the exact same as #ffffff.

THE SHORTHAND HEXADECIMAL FORM

There exists an abbreviated form of hexadecimal colors called the shorthand notation. This method shortens the six digits of hexadecimal color codes into three characters. It only works if every two digits in a pair are identical. For example, #FF77AA becomes #F7A and #33CCEE can be written as #3CE.

For this method to work, every two digits that compose a pair must be the same. As such, #FF8811 can be shortened but #F7C63D cannot.

COLORS BY RGB VALUE

The second method used to indicate a color is the **RGB scale**.

To be fair, it's not so much a different method as an alternative notation of the hexadecimal form. Both use the RGB (Red-Green-Blue) color model, although this time we're not bothering with hexadecimals.

The RGB method just uses regular decimals to designate a specific color. Here is an example of its syntax.

```
h1 { color: rgb(255, 0, 0); }
```

This will turn your titles red.

The number 255 is simply the decimal form of FF. We can write red, #FF0000, #F00 or rgb(255, 0, 0) for the same effect. Similarly, any hex triplet can easily be converted to RGB with simple math. The color #FFBA00 becomes rgb(0, 186, 255). As B (11) x 16 + A (10) = 186.

Try it yourself.

```
p { color: #00BAFF; }

em { color: rgb(0, 186, 255); }
```

Different syntax, same color.

 But what's the point of the RGB notation if it's the same as the hexadecimal form?

It's a matter of preference. The hex format is often favored as it is easily readable and more compact. It's always good to know both, and there is a particular instance where it's more convenient to use the RGB representation.

We'll learn more about this case a bit further on in this chapter. In addition, you can also find the RGB value of any color simply by using a graphics editor such as Photoshop.

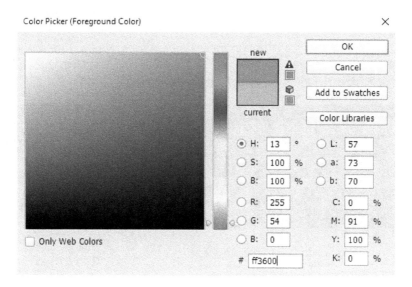

The RGB scale in Photoshop

BACKGROUND COLOR

We saw how to change the text color on our web page in CSS.

But how do we modify the background color? To indicate a background color you just use the `background-color` property. It works in the exact same way as `color`, meaning you can specify a color by typing its name, its RGB value or by using the hexadecimal notation.

Let's try it out.

```
body
{
    background-color: black;
    color: white;
}
```

Which should give you the following result.

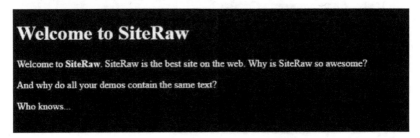

A darker background with CSS

There is nothing very complicated about this code, it simply turns the background black and the text white.

 But why are the title and text white as well? The `color` property is only changed on the `<body>` tag!

Good point.

This is called **inheritance** and is a main feature of CSS. Inheritance is the process by which properties are passed from parent to child elements. In the case of nested tags, once a style is applied to an element, every other element within it will inherit the same style.

In our example, since the header <h1> and the paragraphs <p> are inside the body tag <body>, they are both rendered with the same properties.

 If you want to apply a style to every element in your web page as in our demonstration, you can apply it to either the root <html> or the <body> tag. It's a matter of preference.

 So from now on every text I write on my web page will be white?

Not necessarily. If you apply a new style to one of the child elements, the new properties will take precedence over the inherited style. For the sake of demonstration let's add a few properties to our example.

```
body
{
    background-color: black;
    color: white;
}

h1, strong
{
    text-decoration: underline;
    color: orangered;
}
```

The most specific definition takes precedence, so the <strong> and <h1> tags will be orange while any other text remains white.

This is true for every CSS property, not just for text and background colors.

CSS3 GRADIENTS

Alright... changing the background color was pretty cool. But what about adding a gradient? Prior to CSS3 you had to use images to get a transition between two or more colors, an effect you can now attain simply with the background-image property.

LINEAR GRADIENTS

A **linear or axial color gradient** is the most common type of gradient you will come across. As it name suggests it provides a transition between two or more colors through a linear axis.

Here is the basic CSS blueprint for a background linear gradient.

```
background-image: linear-gradient(direction,
color1, color2);
```

The default direction is from top to bottom. For example.

```
background-image: linear-gradient(yellow,
orange);
```

As mentioned above, linear gradients are by default vertical and from top to bottom.

If you want to change that, you can very easily add a direction value either by typing it out or by providing an angle in standard geometrical degrees.

```
background-image: linear-gradient(to right,
deepskyblue, lightskyblue);

background-image: linear-gradient(90deg,
deepskyblue, lightskyblue);
```

These two lines render the exact same gradient. You can also indicate a diagonal direction as follows.

```
background-image: linear-gradient(to bottom
right, orange, yellow);
```

That covers pretty much every type of dual-colored linear gradient you will come across. But what if you want to have more than two colors? All you need to do is add the supplementary colors at the end of the code.

```
background-image: linear-gradient(skyblue,
yellow, red);
```

This will give you a top to bottom (default as unspecified) three color linear gradient. You can of course use as many colors as you want and modify the direction of the gradient as we've seen previously.

RADIAL GRADIENTS

A **radial gradient** is very similar to a linear gradient as they both produce a dynamic transition between two or more colors. In simple terms, a radial gradient is an ellipse or a circle that possesses one color at the edge and another at the center. Colors are calculated by linear interpolation based on distance from the center. The syntax is very close to that of the linear gradient as the same `background-image` property is used.

```
background-image: radial-gradient(shape,
color1, color2);
```

The default shape is the ellipse. The first color is the color at the center and the last color is the one closest to the edges.

Let's try it out.

```
background-image: radial-gradient(yellow,
orangered);
```

As I said, the default shape is an ellipse. But you can also make it a circle if you want. The difference between the ellipse and the circle is that the latter's center is equidistant from every point. This means that for a given circle, the radius will always be the same and the eccentricity will be 0. Here is how to create a circular radial gradient in CSS.

```
background-image: radial-gradient(circle,
yellow, orangered);
```

This covers everything you need to know about gradients in CSS.

BACKGROUND IMAGE

Just as we can change the background color of a page, or an element thereof, we can also add a background image. You can either add a background image to your entire page or to a specific element, such as a title or a text link. We will also see how we can repeat the background in a mosaic pattern or have it "follow" the user as he scrolls down the page.

ADDING A BACKGROUND IMAGE

Unsurprisingly, the CSS property you need to apply a background image is no other than `background-image`. We already saw this property when dealing with gradients and its use with images is similar enough. The only real difference is in the value of this property. Instead of being the CSS function `linear-gradient` or `radial-gradient`, we'll be using the `url` function with the path to the image you want as a background.

For example.

```
body { background-image: url("siteraw.png"); }
```

Remember that for this code to work, the image siteraw.png must be in the same folder as your CSS file.

197

The background image doesn't have to be in PNG, it could also be a JPG or GIF image as we learned in our Inserting images chapter.

 A common mistake is to write the path to the image relative to the .html file. If your image doesn't load, make sure that the path is relative to the .css file. In our example, since the .html and .css files are in the same folder the image path is identical in both cases.

BACKGROUND IMAGE PROPERTIES

The `background-image` property is by itself very versatile: you can use it for both gradients and background images. But there are also several other CSS features that can supplement it and allow you to modify the behavior of your background image even further.

Here are a few of these features.

BACKGROUND ATTACHMENT

The first property we'll learn about is `background-attachment`. As its name suggests, it is used to "attach" the background to the page or to the element to which it is applied.

Here are the two values it can take:

- scroll : the background will scroll with the rest of the page (default)
- fixed : the background will remain fixed with regard to the viewport

Let's try it out with our example.

```
body
{
    background-image: url("siteraw.png");
    background-attachment: fixed;
}
```

To see the effect you need a sufficient amount of content for the vertical scrollbars to appear on your browser. If you don't have them, try adding some text or reducing the window size.

BACKGROUND REPEAT

By default, if the background image is smaller than the viewport, it will be repeated in a mosaic pattern either horizontally, vertically or both depending on the size of the image and the user's screen resolution. For instance.

CSS background repeat

This behavior can be changed with the background-repeat property. Here are the values it can take.

- repeat : the image will be repeated both ways (default)
- repeat-x : the image will be repeated horizontally
- repeat-y : the image will be repeated vertically
- no-repeat : the background won't be repeated

Example of use.

```
body
{
    background-image: url("siteraw.png");
    background-repeat: no-repeat;
}
```

BACKGROUND SIZE

By default, the background will take the exact size of your image. But you can also specify a value with the background-size property. You can either define an identical value for both the height and width, or list them separately starting with the width.

```
background-size: 50%;
/* Both the height and width will be halved
from their original values */

background-size: 300px 450px;
/* Width: 300px, Height: 450px */
```

To indicate a length value, you can use inches, pixels, percentages or any other unit we saw in the Text formatting chapter. If you want either the height or the width to scale automatically with the image size, simply use the `auto` value. This is the default value of the background-size property.

```
background-size: auto auto;
```

BACKGROUND POSITION

The last property we'll cover concerns the position of the background image. You can specify how the background image should be positioned with background-position. This property is only interesting if you set background-repeat to no-repeat (a non-repeating background).

Here are the values it can take.

- `top` : at the top
- `bottom` : at the bottom
- `left` : to the left
- `right` : to the right
- `center` : centered

These values can be combined.

To align your background image with the top right corner, you would write.

```
background-position: top right;
```

Instead of the predefined values listed above, you can also specify a pair of lengths to represent the position of the background image relative to the top left corner of the page or of the element to which it is applied, starting from the left.

```
background-position: 35px 50px;
```

The code shown above will position your background image to the top left, with a 35 pixel offset from the left and a 50 pixel offset from the top.

THE BACKGROUND SUPER-PROPERTY

We discovered quite a few ways to modify our background, whether by filling it with a color, adding an image or even tempering with its size, attachment and position. The only issue is that all this can get quite inconvenient to write down each time we decide to adjust our background. Consider the following code.

```
body
{
    background-color: #f00;
    background-image: url("siteraw.png");
    background-repeat: no-repeat;
    background-attachment: fixed;
    background-position: top right;
}
```

Rather lengthy. But what if I told you there was a way to shorten everything I just wrote into one single CSS property? It's entirely feasible with the background super-property. Shorthand properties or "super-properties" are used to minimize syntax by combining the values of several related properties.

Here is how it works.

```
background: <color> <image> <repeat>
<attachment> <position>;
```

The order in which the values are placed is important. Going back to our example, using the background super-property transforms our code into the following.

```
background: #f00 url("siteraw.png") no-repeat
fixed top right;
```

You don't have to use every property. Those left unspecified will simply take their default value. For example, if you only wanted a background color and a background image you would write.

```
background: #f00 url("siteraw.png");
```

If for any reason the background image can't be loaded, the background color will be shown instead. This is a common CSS practice.

Shorthand properties or super-properties are very useful for condensing and simplifying your CSS code. For now we only learned about background, but we will see many others in this tutorial.

TRANSPARENCY

So now that we learned how to colorize our text, how to change background colors and even how to insert a background image... what could there possibly be left in this chapter? If you guessed **transparency**, that only proves you know how to read titles. Congratulations. There are two ways to handle transparency in CSS: the **opacity method** and the **RGBa notation**. While they are very similar in theory, they both have distinct practical uses.

THE OPACITY METHOD

The opacity method makes use of the opacity property. Its value is a decimal between 0 and 1:

- a value of 1 will make the element completely opaque (default)
- a value of 0 will make the element completely transparent

Anything in between will be adjusted accordingly. As such, an opacity of 0.7 will produce a 70% opaque (and 30% transparent) element. Here is how it can be used.

```
p { opacity: 0.7; }
```

For a more visually revealing example have a look at the following code.

```
body
{
    background: #000;
    color: #fff;
}

p
{
    background: orangered;
    opacity: 0.5;
}
```

The <body> element has a black background and white text. The opacity decimal isn't specified so it will take the default, 100% opaque value. On the other hand, we set the opacity for the <p> tag to 50%. You can see the result yourselves: the paragraphs are half transparent.

 But why is the text transparent? What if I only want the background to blend in with the rest of the page?

Good point.

Applying the opacity property to an item will affect every element contained within the item including text, images and even other blocks of content. If you want only the background color to be transparent you should use the RGBa notation that we're going to find out about.

THE RGBA NOTATION

At the beginning of this chapter, when we were introducing the different methods to specify colors, I stated that the hex format was usually preferred except for one case where the RGB notation was more convenient. This is what I was talking about: the RGBa notation. It's the same as the RGB notation with an additional setting called alpha channel, which handles transparency. This fourth component controls the level of transparency in the same way as the opacity property we saw above: a value of 1 will make the color opaque, a value of 0 will make it completely transparent (invisible).

Let's give it a try.

```
p
{
    background-color: rgb(255, 0, 0);
    /* A red background */

    background-color: rgba(255, 0, 0, 0.5);
    /* A semi-transparent red */
}
```

Unlike with `opacity`, only the background color will be affected by the transparency levels.

This concludes the chapter on colors and backgrounds.

BORDERS AND SHADOWS

In the last chapter we learned how to adjust the colors and backgrounds of our elements. But CSS allows you much more options to stylize your site and improve your web design. In this chapter, we're going to take a deeper look at the borders and shadowing effects, the latter of which can be applied both to block elements as well as the text contained within them. Everything we learned during the previous chapter will come in handy as borders and shadows make use of colors and function in a somewhat comparable way to backgrounds.

Let's start with borders.

BORDERS

The CSS language offers you a wide selection of properties to decorate your elements with borders.

The three main properties we will use are `border-width`, `border-style` and `border-color` which respectively control the width, style and color of your borders. Here is how they work.

The **border width** specifies the size of your border and takes a length value. I recommend using pixels as a unit but feel free to use any of the length units we saw in the Text formatting chapter. The **border color** is the color of your border. As we learned in the previous chapter, you can either type the color's name (e.g. red), its hexadecimal code (e.g. #f00) or its RGB value (e.g. rgb(255, 0, 0)). The **border style** is a bit different. You have several options available to customize your border depending on the type of effect you're going after. You can choose between a straight line, a dashed line or even a dotted line.

Here are the values it can take:

- `solid` : a single solid line
- `dashed` : a dashed line
- `dotted` : a dotted line
- `double` : a double solid line
- `groove` : a grooved line
- `ridge` : a ridged line
- `inset` : a 3D inset line
- `outset` : a 3D outset line
- `none` : no border (default)

To give you a clear idea of the different effects you can take a look the following graphic.

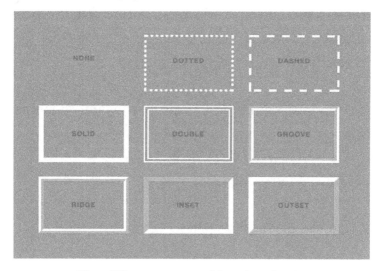

The different types of borders in CSS

Let's test these new properties.

```
p
{
    border-width: 3px;
    border-style: dashed;
    border-color: deeppink;
}
```

You can of course experiment with these properties by modifying their values as much as you wish.

 Why do I need three properties to use borders in CSS? One should be enough!

Indeed, having to define three properties for a single element's borders can quickly make your code lengthy and redundant. Luckily, CSS allows you to use the border super-property which combines all three properties we just discovered. Remember super-properties from the previous chapter? Super-properties or shorthand properties allow you to condense multiple CSS properties into a single line of code.

Here is how border works.

```
border: <border-width> <border-style> <border-color>;
```

If we were to revise our example to make use this new super-property.

```
p { border: 3px dashed deeppink; }
```

This code produces the exact same result as the longer one shown a bit higher up.

INDIVIDUAL BORDERS

As of now we learned how to adjust the borders around a given HTML element. But you may have noticed that the border super-property affects every side of the rectangular block.

In reality, each element possesses four individual borders for each geometric side (top, bottom, left, right). You can decorate them separately with these four super-properties.

- `border-top` : the top border
- `border-right` : the right border
- `border-bottom` : the bottom border
- `border-left` : the left border

While they only apply their style to a single side, they are super-properties and work in the same way as border. Here is how you can use them.

```
p
{
        border-top: 5px solid deeppink;
        border-right: 20px groove red;
        border-bottom: 5px solid deepskyblue;
        border-left: 20px double orangered;
}
```

These are in fact super-properties. In the same way that `border` combines the properties `border-width`, `border-style` and `border-color`, you can also write `border-top-width` or `border-left-style`. For example.

```
p
{
        border: 5px solid orangered;
        border-top-color: deeppink;
        border-bottom-style: double;
        border-bottom-color: deepskyblue;
}
```

Here are some of the results you can obtain with a little imagination.

CSS different borders

You don't have to apply a border to every side. You can add a single border above or below your element if you want using the appropriate CSS property.

ROUNDED BORDERS

So basic CSS borders are pretty cool. But since CSS3 came around, you can go even further in customizing your borders with the **rounded border** feature.

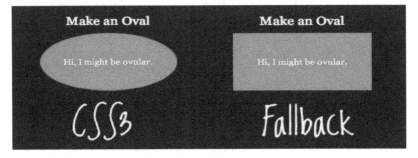

Rounded borders with CSS

The property you will need is `border-radius` and it takes between one and four values. The values represent the radius ("amount of roundness") of each corner of the borders or background belonging to your element. Let's start with the simplest case. If you indicate only one value, every corner will have the same radius.

```
border-radius: 15px;
```

The effect is only seen if you first define a border, as shown in the image below.

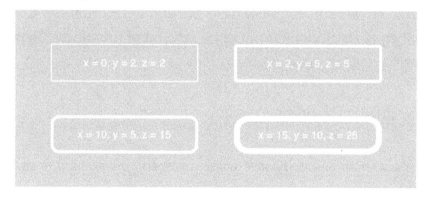

Border radius example

The rounded effect works on borders but also on backgrounds.

```
p
{
    background-color: orangered;
    border-radius: 15px;
}
```

Here is an example.

A green, padded button with white link text.

With rounded corners, it makes
you want to push it just a little bit more, right?

A background with rounded corners

This covers the simplest case of rounded borders in CSS: when every corner has the same amount of roundness. There are of course many more options.

MULTIPLE RADIUS VALUES

You can also specify the radius of each corner. In this case the property border-radius will take four values.

```
border-radius: 10px 25px 10px 25px;
```

These values correspond to the four corners in this order:

- top left
- top right
- bottom right
- bottom left

You just have to remember that it starts from the top left corner and goes clockwise.

 A simple rule of CSS: anytime you are dealing with values for different geometrical points (or sides), the order is always a clockwise rotation usually starting from the top.

You don't have to enter exactly four values either. Here are the different scenarios based on the number of values you indicate.

1 ◻ 2 / 4 3	1 2 3 4 border-radius: 1px 2px 3px 4px;
1 ◻ 2 / 2 3	1 2 3 border-radius: 1px 2px 3px;
1 ◻ 2 / 2 1	1 2 border-radius: 1px 2px;
1 ◻ 1 / 1 1	1 border-radius: 1px;

The border-radius property

In practice, you only need to remember the first and last rule (one and four values) as they are the most common.

ELLIPTIC CORNERS

There is one last feature of the `border-radius` shorthand property that we're left to discover: how to create elliptic corners. To create elliptic curves you must specify two values per corner, separated by a slash character (/). The first value is the horizontal radius and the second is the vertical radius.

```
border-radius: 20px / 10px;
```

Having different values is what creates the elliptic curve. You can see a few results below.

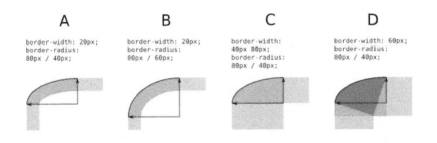

Elliptic corners in CSS

This covers every use of rounded borders in CSS.

BOX SHADOW

Adding a shadowing effect is one of the latest features of CSS3. Since a picture is worth a thousand words, this is an example of the effect you can obtain with CSS.

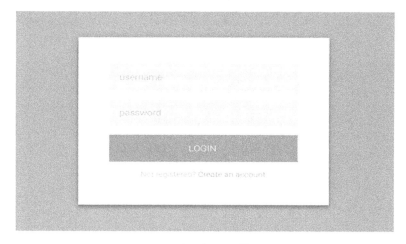

CSS shadow effect

Pretty cool? So let's learn how to add this effect to some of our elements. The property you will need is box-shadow. It takes anywhere between two and five values. Two is the strict minimum, representing the horizontal and vertical offset of the shadow. Here is an example.

```
div { box-shadow: 5px 5px; }
```

This is the simplest and most straightforward use of this property. A horizontal offset of 5 pixels and a vertical offset of 5 pixels. The result of this code is shown in the example A of the figure below.

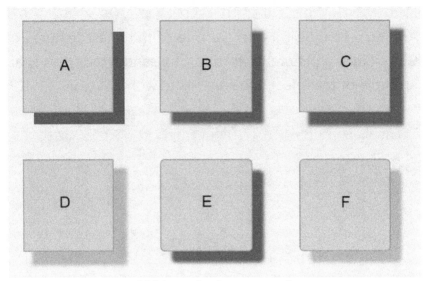

CSS box shadow example

As you may have guessed from the image, there are many more ways to customize your shadows using this property. But to do so we will need all five values not just the two mandatory ones that we used in our demonstration. Here are the five values the box-shadow property can include.

- **Horizontal offset** (mandatory). The horizontal distance between the shadow and the element. In other words the horizontal "size" of the shadow. A positive value will shift the shadow to the right whereas a negative value will shift it to the left.
- **Vertical offset** (mandatory). The vertical distance between the shadow and the element. In other words the vertical "size" of the shadow. A positive value will shift the shadow to the bottom whereas a negative value will shift it to the top.

- **Blur radius** (optional). The amount of blur applied to the shadow. By default it is worth 0, making the shadow the sharpest it can be.
- **Spread radius** (optional). The spread of the shadow relative to the size of the element.
- **Color** (optional). The color of the shadow. If left unspecified it will usually be the same color as that of the text inside the element.

The first four are length values and, with the exception of the blur radius, they all support negative values. Let's try it out.

```
h1
{
    background: deeppink;
    box-shadow: 5px -5px 0 0 black;
}

div
{
    background: orangered;
    box-shadow: -7px 10px 5px -5px deepskyblue;
}
```

You can play around with this property until you get the effect that you want.

INNER SHADOWS

Rather than a drop shadow, you can create an inset shadow simply by adding the `inset` keyword before or after the other values.

```
box-shadow: inset 5px 5px 3px 0 #f00;
```

Here are some of the results you can obtain by playing around with box shadows.

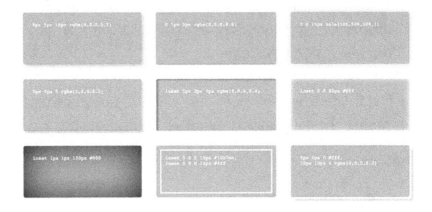

CSS shadow examples

The inner shadow effect is most visible on the bottom three examples.

TEXT SHADOW

We just learned how to apply box shadows to our web page's elements with CSS. But there is another type of shadow we can use, the **text shadow**. As it's name implies, it adds a shadowing effect not to the element itself but to each letter of the text.

Here is a demonstration.

CSS text shadow demonstration

The property we need to handle text shadowing is `text-shadow`. Here are the values it accepts.

- **Horizontal offset** (mandatory). The horizontal distance between the shadow and the text. In other words the horizontal "length" of the shadow. A positive value will shift the shadow to the right whereas a negative value will shift it to the left.
- **Vertical offset** (mandatory). The vertical distance between the shadow and the text. In other words the vertical "length" of the shadow. A positive value will shift the shadow to the bottom whereas a negative value will shift it to the top.
- **Blur radius** (optional). The amount of blur applied to the shadow. By default it is worth 0, making the shadow the sharpest it can be.

- **Color** (optional). The color of the shadow. The default color will depend on the browser.

As you can see, these are very similar to the values of the box-shadow property except for the spread radius option which is not used for text shadows. This means that text-shadow will have at most four values. Here is an example of a very simple text shadow effect.

```
text-shadow: 3px 3px;
```

And a slightly more advanced one.

```
text-shadow: 5px 5px 7px #f00;
```

With a little creativity, you can easily create very cool text effect with just this property.

CSS text shadow effect

Multiple shadows

Lastly, you should know that you can easily create multiple shadows by separating them with a comma. This works both for box shadows and text shadows. Demonstration.

```
div
{
    box-shadow: 5px 5px 0 0 #f0f, -3px -3px 1px 2px #f00;
    text-shadow: 1px 1px 1px #000, 3px 3px 5px #f00;
}
```

Here are some of the effects you can obtain by using multiple shadows.

HTML page with titles

This concludes our chapter on borders and shadows in CSS.

PSEUDO CLASS SELECTORS

P seudo-classes are one of the strong points of CSS: they allow you to dynamically modify the appearance of the elements of your website. In other words, you can change the shape of your items and add dynamic effects to your pages even after they are loaded by the browser. We are not going to learn new CSS properties in this chapter. You already know quite a lot of them by now. We will rather see how to apply them at specific times or places. For example, we will learn how to change the appearance of a hyperlink when the visitor moves his mouse over it or when it is clicked by the user. All these elements allow you to add even more dynamism to your website. This is what pseudo **class selectors** are for.

WHAT IS A PSEUDO-CLASS

Since we'll be talking about pseudo-classes in this chapter

it makes sense to define what these are before going into more concrete examples of how they work.

Pseudo-classes or pseudo-class selectors are keywords added to CSS selectors in order to specify a special state of the selected element. As a small revision before getting into anything new, here are how CSS selectors work.

```
selector
{
    property: value;
}
```

Pseudo-classes allow you to you apply a style to an element in relation to external factors like the history of the navigator, the status of its content or the position of the mouse. To use a pseudo-class you simply add a colon (:) to the selector, followed by the name of the pseudo-class.

```
selector:pseudo-class
{
    property: value;
}
```

You can apply pseudo-classes to any type of selector we discovered in the Setting up CSS chapter: tag names, classes or IDs.

```
tag:pseudo-class { } /* Tag name selector */
.class:pseudo-class { } /* Class selector */
#id:pseudo-class { } /* ID selector */
```

You can also select elements within the item affected by the pseudo-class.

```
div:pseudo-class a { property: value; }
```

We will go into more detail when we learn about each individual pseudo-class selector.

WHEN HOVERING

As you may have guessed, the :pseudo-class keyword we used until now in our examples is not an actual pseudo-class selector. Real pseudo-classes have an actual function. The first one that we we'll discovered is by far the most common, the :hover pseudo-class. It's very often used on hyperlinks but can otherwise be applied to any HTML element or CSS selector of your choosing. The syntax is exactly the same as what we saw in our examples.

```
a:hover
{
    color: red;
}
```

The :hover pseudo-class affects any element determined by the selector and adds the condition of a mouse over.

In our example, hyperlinks will be displayed in red when the user moves his pointer over the link (and will revert back to default when the pointer is not longer on the link). Keep in mind that these attributes will take precedence over any regular CSS style. Here is an example.

```
a
{
    text-decoration: none;
    color: blue;
}

a:hover
{
    text-decoration: underline;
    color: red;
}
```

The color of the link changes on a mouse over and an underline is added. With a little imagination you can add any effect you want with this pseudo-class. Remember when I said that you could also select elements contained within the item affected by the pseudo-class? Let's give it a try with :hover, see below for the HTML code.

```
<ul>
    <li>Do you know about <a href="http://www.
siteraw.com">SiteRaw</a>? It's the <strong>best
site</strong> on the web.</li>
    <li>Do you also know about <a
href="http://www.siteraw.com">SiteRaw</a>? It's
the second <strong>best site</strong> on the
web.</li>
    <li>And don't forget <a href="http://www.
siteraw.com">SiteRaw</a>. It's in the top five
<strong>best sites</strong> ever.</li>
    </ul>
```

And the associated CSS.

```
li:hover strong
{
    color: red;
    font-style: italic;
}
```

This works just like the first examples, with the exception that the <strong> emphasis is highlighted regardless of where you point your mouse as long as it's on the same horizontal line as the <li> bullet. The CSS code literally means "whenever the user points his mouse inside a <li> tag, only add the following style to the <strong> element". I suggest you play around with this pseudo-class and get intuitive with the various ways it can add dynamism to your web pages.

CLICKING, SELECTING AND VISITED

We just learned about the :hover pseudo-class which allows you to dynamically change the style of an element when the user drags his mouse pointer over it. But CSS allows you to interact even more finely with the different states of your elements.

WHEN CLICKED

The :active pseudo-format allows you to apply a particular

style to an element when it's clicked by the user. In practice, it's mostly used on hyperlinks. This effect is only activated when the user clicks on the element so the new appearance won't be visible for very long. For example, you can change the color of your links (or paragraphs or titles).

```
a:active { color: red; }
```

This will turn your links red only when clicked by the user.

WHEN FOCUSED

The :focus pseudo-class applies a style when the element is selected. This is slightly different from :active as it affects any element that has gained focus. Let's try it out on hyperlinks.

```
a:focus { color: red; }
```

The best way to see this effect is to keep pressing Tab until one of the affected links acquires focus.

 This pseudo-class works best on a few HTML tags that we haven't seen yet such as form elements. Don't worry, we'll cover them soon enough in this tutorial.

WHEN VISITED

You can assign a specific style to a link pointing to a page that has already been viewed by the user. By default and when no style is defined, the browser automatically colors visited links in purple. Let's make it red instead.

```
a:visited { color: red; }
```

Aside from search engines like Google and Bing, most websites don't use this feature as it gets confusing for the user. If you don't want visited links to be distinguishable for unvisited ones, you only need to define a style for "standard" links. As long as you provide a style for "standard" links via the a selector, visited links will automatically inherit the associated properties unless overwritten by the :visited pseudo-class. More on this below.

WHEN UNVISITED

If you want your style only to affect unvisited links you can use the :link pseudo-class. The properties defined will not be inherited by :visited.

```
a:link { color: red; }
a:visited { color: red; }
```

The above code is equivalent to the one below.

```
a { color: red; }
```

This pseudo-class also has a specificity: it only applies to hyperlinks. If you remember our chapter on Creating links, we introduced the <a> tag as the anchor element. It only becomes a hyperlink if a href attribute is specified.

BEFORE AND AFTER

The pseudo-formats we are going to see now are very interesting and are a bit different from what we are used to doing in CSS. Imagine that you have a web page in the form of a Q&A (Questions and Answers). Our HTML code would look something like this.

```
<p class="question">What is SiteRaw</p>

<p>The best site on the web.</p>

[...]

<p class="question">Why is SiteRaw so awesome</p>

<p>I don't know.</p>
```

The number of questions and answers could be anywhere between 10 and 30. Now suppose that I'm a lazy webmaster (trust me there are many lazy webmasters around) and I want to add the text "Question: ..." before each question, just to make it more readable.

Also, I'm a punctuation noob and I forgot the question marks so we'll have to add those at the end as well. We could of course manually edit the questions to add what we want directly in the HTML code. But since we are lazy, let's look at a way we can automate this insertion instead.

CSS PSEUDO-ELEMENTS

To do so we are going to use the two following pseudo-elements, `::before` and `::after`.

 Pseudo-elements? I thought we were talking about pseudo-classes?

They are, for all intents and purposes, exactly the same. Prior to CSS3 there was in fact no distinction between one and the other. In short, pseudo-classes act as *ways to define the special states of an item* whereas pseudo-element *create new virtual elements.*

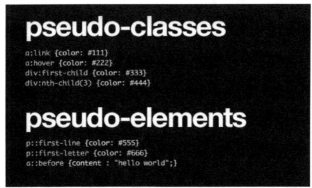

CSS pseudo-elements

You will notice that pseudo-elements are preceded by two colons : : rather than one :. This is a new CSS3 convention to differentiate the two. Other than that, pseudo-elements work in the exact same way as pseudo-classes.

```
.question::before { content: "Question: "; }

.question::after { content: "?"; }
```

This property will insert content into the HTML page without it being in the DOM (Document Object Model). It's quite different from what we've seen until now and is somewhat of an exception in CSS. You're not limited to using only content with the : :before and : :after pseudo-elements either. Let's go back to our example.

```
.question
{
    color: blue;
    font-style: italic;
}

.question::before
{
    content: "Question: ";
    font-weight: bold;
    text-decoration: underline;
}

.question::after { content: "?"; }
```

It's also possible to add an image instead of text with the : :before and : :after pseudo-elements.

We still use the `content` property but this time to indicate the path to the image with the `url` function.

```
.question::before { content: url("question.png"); }
```

Let's try it out.

Welcome to SiteRaw

What is SiteRaw?

The best site on the web.

Is SiteRaw really the best site ever?

Probably.

Why is SiteRaw so awesome?

I don't know.

Pseudo-elements with an image

Keep in my these are just examples, and you can use both pseudo-classes and pseudo-elements to decorate your site in the way you want.

PART III

WEBSITE CREATION

STRUCTURE YOUR PAGE

This is the first chapter of the third part of our tutorial on how to create a website with HTML and CSS. Having learned about both the HTML and the CSS languages in the two previous parts, all that's left to do is to put them together to start building our website. You may have notice that while we know how to insert element with HTML and even stylize them thanks to CSS, our pages still don't look quite like what we're used to seeing on websites. That's completely normal. Keep reading to find out why. In this chapter we will learn how to structure our web pages in the best way possible.

WEBPAGE STRUCTURE

Most websites aren't that original. Sure, they all seem to have different designs and decorations, but if you think about it for a few minutes you'll realize that the core of nearly every site remains identical.

When you remove every dispensable and purely cosmetic feature, there are four elements that you will find on almost every website you visit.

- a header
- a navigation menu
- a central content area
- a footer

Some are necessary for smooth web browsing (navigation menu) while others are conventionally expected on a website. If we were to draw a blueprint that would fit most web pages, we would get something like this.

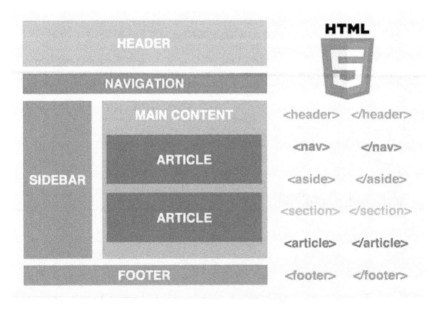

HTML page with titles

The four distinct sections are easily recognizable. Pick any website you want, including this one (www.siteraw.com), and chances are you'll run into the same structure. They will usually have very different content, functionality and look and feel but they'll almost all follow the same common pattern.

HTML STRUCTURAL TAGS

Now is the time to answer the age old question: how do we translate that blueprint into readable and workable HTML code?

Prior to HTML5 there was only one tag for handling web page anatomy: <div> (or <table> even before that). Besides being repetitive, the problem with using only one tag for structural purposes is that <div> carries no semantics. While human readers can identify the distinct elements thanks to CSS styles (and a bit of experience and intuition), browsers, screen readers and robots can't... which defeats the purpose of having HTML as a semantic language.

Thankfully this inconvenience has been since then resolved, as HTML5 saw the apparition of six new tags designed specifically for building the framework of your website.

These are called HTML structural elements and are as follows.

- `<header>`: Contains the header content of a site.
- `<footer>`: Contains the footer content of a site.
- `<nav>`: Contains the navigation menu or other navigation functionalities of a site.
- `<section>`: Used to either group different articles into different purposes or subjects, or to define the different sections of a single article.
- `<article>`: Contains a standalone piece of content.
- `<aside>`: Contains a block of content that is related to the main content around it, but not central to the flow of it.

Here is what the a standard web page would look like using these tags.

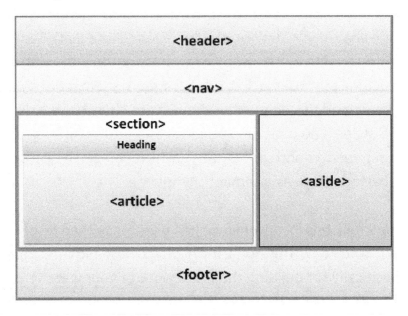

HTML structural elements

We will go into more detailed explanations of each of these new tags, but keep in mind you can use these elements multiple times within the same web page as the figure shows.

THE HEADER ELEMENT

Most websites have a header, it's one of their most recognizable features. Headers can either be a logo, a banner, a slogan or any combination thereof. As mentioned you can have more than one header on each page.

In HTML, the tag used to wrap the header content is <header>. Here is how you would write a simple header code.

```
<header>
    <h1>Welcome to SiteRaw</h1>
</header>
```

You can add whatever content you desire in your header: paragraphs, images, titles of various importance.

THE FOOTER ELEMENT

Unlike the header element, footers are usually placed at the bottom of a web page as their name implies. They usually contain information such as contact information, the author's name, copyright or other legal notices, links to social media profiles and so on.

The tag for the footer content is <footer>. Here is an example.

```
<footer>
    <p>© SiteRaw, the best site on the web.</p>
</footer>
```

THE NAVIGATION ELEMENT

The navigation element features the website's main browsing links and other constructs that bring the visitor to a new page (a search bar for example). You will often find a bulleted browsing menu in the navigation element, either vertical or horizontal. The HTML tag for the navigation content is <nav>. You can see the example of a menu with a bulleted list below.

```
<nav>
    <ul>
        <li><a href="http://www.siteraw.
com">Home</a></li>
        <li><a href="http://www.siteraw.
com">Forum</a></li>
        <li><a href="http://www.siteraw.
com">Contact</a></li>
    </ul>
</nav>
```

THE SECTION ELEMENT

The section element is a more general item containing the main and usually central portion of a web page.

It's a fairly generic element but even so it stills holds more semantic meaning than the regular <div>. You will often find multiple other components included within the section element, as we will learn later on. For now here is a demonstration of the section HTML tag.

```
<section>
    <h1>SiteRaw is awesome</h1>

    <p>SiteRaw is the best site on the web.</p>
</section>
```

Keep in mind that you can use these items more than once on your page.

THE SECTION ELEMENT

We now saw the four main structural elements of HTML.

 Four? But you said we were going to learn about six new HTML tags!

That's intentional.

The two tags that we are left with are slightly different as they are generally nested inside another HTML structural element, very often the <section> tag.

The section element is an independent portion of the web page. It can contain headers, footers and navigation menus even if the page already has those itself. Knowing this is important to understand how these new tags work.

THE ARTICLE ELEMENT

The article element is used to classify any type of standalone content, such as news articles (obviously), blog posts, RSS feeds or even images or videos. The rule of thumbs is that if an item of content is suitable to be read or watched on its own, it makes sense to use the article element to mark it. For example, this very tutorial you are currently reading could be marked as an HTML article.

The tag we need for this purpose is <article>. Here is how you can use it.

```
<section>
  <article>
    <h1>SiteRaw is awesome</h1>

    <p>SiteRaw is the best site on the web.</p>
  </article>
</section>
```

You can add several article elements within the same <section> tag as long as it makes semantic sense to do so.

THE ASIDE ELEMENT

The aside element is related to <article> and often goes alongside it. Any content included within it should be additional information that is relevant to the main flow but doesn't fit directly in it. Wiki sites offer good examples of the proper use of the aside element (the panels on the right with information about the author, etc.).

The HTML code for aside elements is <aside>.

```
<aside>
  <h1>About the author</h1>

    <p>SiteRaw was created by... find out never!</p>
</aside>
```

Just as with <article> I recommend nesting the aside element within the section tag.

A section does not necessarily have to contain <article> or <aside> tags. You could create sections only containing paragraphs, or just an <article> and no <aside>. Or even multiple <aside> tags. the possibilities are endless with these HTML elements.

A COMPLETE WEBPAGE

Until now we have mostly talked about the theory behind the use of these tags. It's time to get practical. As a conclusion to this chapter we will be building our first complete web page. Think of this as a heuristic exercise to put test your skills as a web developer. The goal of the exercise is simple: design a web page utilizing every new element we discovered in this chapter. To simplify things even further I've included a diagram of the basic structure we want to build.

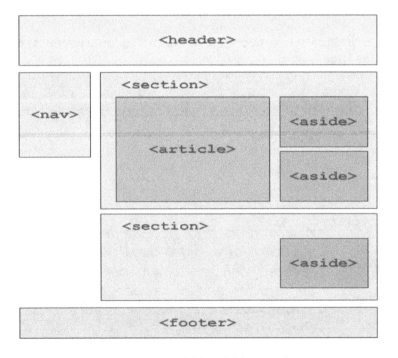

The structure of a webpage

This is just one example of the many ways you can organize your page in HTML.

THE FOUNDATION

For the sake of clarity, our demonstration web page will contain only one occurrence of each HTML structural element. The code below showcases all the tags we've learned about in this chapter.

```
<!DOCTYPE html>
<html>
    <head>
        <meta charset="utf-8" />
        <title>SiteRaw</title>
    </head>
    <body>
        <header>
            [...]
        </header>
        <nav>
            [...]
        </nav>
        <section>
            <article>
                [...]
            </article>

            <aside>
                [...]
            </aside>
        </section>
        <footer>
            [...]
        </footer>
    </body>
</html>
```

This code should help you see how a typical web page is arranged: a header, a navigation menu, a central section and a footer. Of course, our page is empty at the moment. Try filling it with whatever content you want. For our example I simply copied and incorporated the various examples we saw for each element.

```
<!DOCTYPE html>
<html>
    <head>
        <meta charset="utf-8" />
        <title>SiteRaw</title>
    </head>
    <body>
        <header>
            <h1>Welcome to SiteRaw</h1>
        </header>

        <nav>
            <ul>
                <li><a href="http://www.
siteraw.com">Home</a></li>
                <li><a href="http://www.
siteraw.com">Forum</a></li>
                <li><a href="http://www.
siteraw.com">Contact</a></li>
            </ul>
        </nav>

        <section>
            <article>
                <h1>SiteRaw is awesome</h1>

                <p>SiteRaw is the best site on
the web. SiteRaw is the best site on the web.
SiteRaw is the best site on the web.</p>

                <p>SiteRaw is awesome. True
story.</p>
            </article>
```

```
        <aside>
            <h1>About the author</h1>

            <p>SiteRaw was created by...
find out never!</p>
            </aside>
        </section>

        <footer>
            <p>© SiteRaw, the best site on the
web.</p>
        </footer>

    </body>
</html>
```

And here is the result.

Welcome to SiteRaw

- Home
- Forum
- Contact

SiteRaw is awesome

SiteRaw is the best site on the web. SiteRaw is the best site on the web.

SiteRaw is awesome. True story.

About the author

SiteRaw was created by... find out never!

© SiteRaw, the best site on the web.

A basic web page

 This looks nothing like a website! It looks just like what we've been doing until now!

That's perfectly normal. There is no visual difference when using HTML structural elements compared to what we've done until now. HTML is first and foremost a markup language, and the use of these tags is mainly for building a more semantically readable website. It is however entirely possible to format our web page using CSS. You can easily change the design of the web page by applying a few styles to the element we discovered.

A web page with CSS

The HTML code is exactly the same, I only added a bit of CSS.

We'll learn how to do that and much more in the following chapters.

THE CSS BOX MODEL

L et's start with the first question you might ask yourself at the sight of this chapter's title: what is a box model? Perhaps you've realized it already, every HTML element can be represented by a two dimensional rectangular box. In fact, if you look back at the previous chapters, almost all of my diagrams and illustrations conveniently contained at least one such box.

The CSS box model essentially illustrates the fact that a web page can be seen as a succession and stack of multiples "boxes" sometimes also called blocks.

In this chapter we will learn how to interact with these boxes by giving them specific dimensions, placing and aligning them where we want on our page, handling their margins and much more.

These are the basic concepts we need to give our website a true design.

BLOCK AND INLINE ELEMENTS

We've already talked about this distinction before so this will purely be a short review of what we already know. Most HTML tags belong to one o two categories. They can be either:

- block elements such as paragraphs (<p>)
- inline elements such as links (<a>)

In addition to those two there are also several less common level types such as flex or inline-block and even more specific types such as table-cell for tables cells and list-item for each item of a list. Not only are they less frequently used but they can also be considered variations of either the block or inline type.

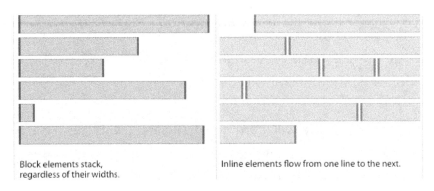

Block elements stack, regardless of their widths.

Inline elements flow from one line to the next.

Inline and block elements

So for now you only need to remember the difference between block and inline elements.

But how do I know which ones are block or inline elements?

Very easily.

- **Block elements** always start on a new line and take up the full width available.
- **Inline elements** don't force a line break and take up only as much width as necessary.

Inline elements are always contained within block elements, which can in turn either be placed next to other blocks or even nested within them. For visualization purposes, this is the behavior of an inline element.

INLINE ELEMENTS FLOW WITH TEXT

PELLENTESQUE HABITANT MORBI TRISTIQUE SENECTUS ET NETUS ET MALESUADA FAMES AC TURPIS EGESTAS. VESTIBULUM │ INLINE ELEMENT │ VITAE, ULTRICIES EGET, TEMPOR SIT AMET, ANTE. DONEC EU LIBERO SIT AMET QUAM EGESTAS SEMPER. AENEAN ULTRICIES MI VITAE EST. MAURIS PLACERAT ELEIFEND LEO.

An inline element

And this is the behavior of a block element.

BLOCK ELEMENTS EXPAND NATURALLY ⟶

AND NATURALLY DROP BELOW OTHER ELEMENTS ↙

A block element

Every HTML tag has a default level type, usually block or inline, but you must remember that these are CSS display behaviors and can therefore be adjusted with the CSS language. We can very easily display links as block elements instead of their default inline, and vice-versa for paragraphs or titles. In fact, we'll learn how to do just that further on in this chapter.

GENERAL PURPOSE TAGS

We already presented these tags in the Setting up CSS chapter so once again this will simply be a review. There are two general purpose tags that you must be aware of in the HTML language, <div> and <span>. The purpose behind these tags is that they carry no semantic meaning, unlike <p> for paragraph or <em> for emphasis.

Given that the entire point of the HTML language is to convey semantic information to the user agent this would seem about as useful as a foam hammer, but they are in fact used quite extensively in conjunction with CSS. Imagine that you need to select a determined portion of HTML content purely for cosmetic reasons. All you need is to apply one of these tags to the desired content and apply a CSS style, often with the `class` (or `id`) selector.

 Yes, we already know that! So what is the difference between <div> and <span> ?

Coincidentally, the only variation between the default display behavior of the two is that <div> is a block element and <span> is an inline element. I'll repeat myself, these are simply default behaviors and can be changed in CSS (although in this case it would make little sense to do so).

- <div> : a block element
- <span> : an inline element

As a last point that bears reiterating, these are generic tags that carry no semantic signification. As such you should only use them when you want your elements to... carry no semantic signification. When there is a more appropriate HTML tag available, use it.

DIMENSIONS IN CSS

Now that were done recapitulating the distinction between block and inline elements let's get back to our box model. Let's start with the dimensions of our boxes. Unlike inline elements whose dimensions are determined dynamically based on the content inside them, block elements tend to have a specific width and height. Unsurprisingly, CSS provides us the following two properties.

- `width`: the width of the element or width of the block
- `height`: the height of the element or height of the block

The values defined can be either absolute, such as with the pixel unit, or relative, such as with percentages.

THE WIDTH

If left unspecified, blocks will fill the entire horizontal area available to them. In other words they will have a width value of 100%. Thanks to these properties we can change the dimensions of our block elements, for example the paragraphs. Try this code.

```
p { width: 50%; }
```

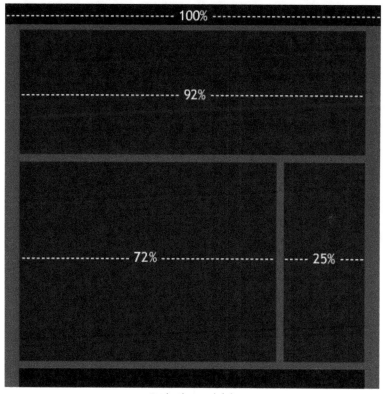

Relative width

When working with relative sizes such as percentages, it's important to remember that the size value of an item is based on the dimensions of its parent element. This is particularly relevant in the case of nested tags. Take the following code.

```
div { width: 50%; }
div p { width: 50%; }
```

Both the <div> element and the paragraph contained within it have their respective widths set to 50%.

And yet, here is the result.

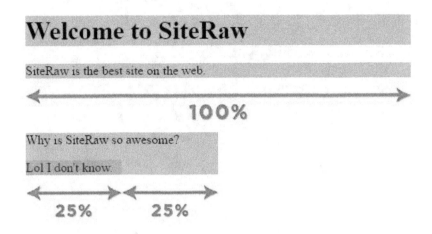

A paragraph inside another block

What happened? When you apply a relative value to the dimensions of one of your blocks, the actual size will be determined according to the dimensions of the parent element. In our case the final width of the paragraph isn't 50% of the entire page, but 50% of the <div> element which itself takes up 50% of the page. In other words 50% of 50% which makes it 25%, as shown in the example.

 That seems overly complicated! Can't we just use regular lengths in pixels or inches?

It's actually very intuitive once you start seeing the design of web pages in terms of boxes.

Relative sizes are very useful for creating designs that automatically adapt themselves to the screen resolution of the visitor. But to answer your question, it's entirely possible to specify an absolute length value rather than a relative size.

```
p { width: 250px; }
```

In this case the paragraphs will always be 250 pixels wide, irrelevant of the dimensions of the parent element or the user's screen size.

THE HEIGHT

Unlike for width where we had two different behaviors for block and inline elements, there is no such distinction with the height property. All HTML elements will by default only fill as much vertical space as necessary. A block element only expands to its parent's width but not to the parent's height. This can lead to a few issues such as the following.

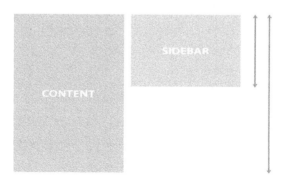

Different heights in CSS

There is an obvious disparity in heights between the two elements. How can we fix that? It's just a matter of applying an identical value to the height property of both elements. Let's try with this code.

```
p { height: 300px; }
```

This should fix the heights of our boxes.

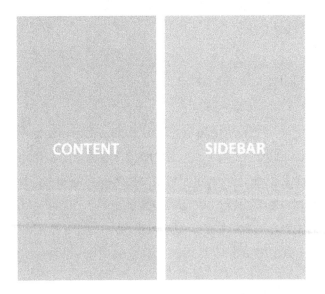

Two elements with the same height

This is particularly useful when you need to align several elements on the horizontal axis, such as with a menu bar or with equal height columns. Every item needs to have the same vertical size for the effect to work.

As with `width`, you can enter either an absolute or a relative value for the `height` property.

MINIMUM AND MAXIMUM

In addition to what we just saw, you can also indicate a block's minimum and maximum dimensions with CSS. This is only useful if you specify relative values for the `height` and `width` properties, otherwise the size doesn't change dynamically and there is therefore no distinct minimum and maximum. There are four CSS properties you need to know of to achieve this effect.

- `min-height` : the minimum height
- `min-width` : the minimum width
- `max-height` : the maximum height
- `max-width` : the maximum width

Two for the minimum and two for the maximum. Or two for the height and two for the width depending on how you choose to memorize them. Here is how you can use these properties.

```
p
{
    width: 75%;
    min-width: 400px;
}
```

This code means your paragraphs should occupy 75% of the horizontal space available if possible, but always be at least 400 pixels wide. Try changing the width of your browser window to see the effect in action (add a background color to the paragraphs to make them stand out). The size of the block should follow that of the browser window until it reaches a certain minimum... 400 pixels.

MARGINS AND PADDING

We know that every visible HTML element has a set of dimensions. If you think of web design in terms of boxes, it makes sense to assume that the dimensions of one "box" are the same as the dimensions of the element it represents. Let's take an example. My paragraphs are 400 pixels wide. They are then displayed as 400 pixel wide boxes, right?

 Right!

Wrong.

 Why would that not be true? It doesn't make any sense!

It's not necessarily a false statement but it's certainly not always the case depending on several factors. We already know one from one of our previous chapters: **borders**. HTML elements may or may not have borders surrounding it.

So if the paragraphs are 400 pixels wide and the borders are 10 pixels wide on all sides, the total width of the "box" will be 420 pixels (10 + 400 + 10). It's important to remember that dimensions in CSS are additive not subtractive. The size of the box is not invariably that of the element it wraps around.

You also have to account for several other factors. There are four parts that compose a CSS box: the content, its borders and its margins.

 That's only three! Stop trying to teach us arithmetics if you can't even count.

That's because there are two types of margins in CSS.

There is an inner margin called padding and an outer margin that is mostly just called margin.

- padding: the inner margin, between content and border
- margin: the outer margin, outside of the border

If you need a more visual example look at the figure below.

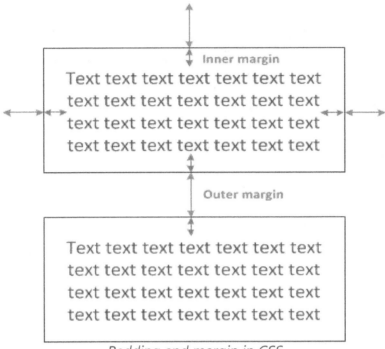

Padding and margin in CSS

We now know all four parts that compose the CSS box model. In order, from the center to the periphery:

- the content
- the padding
- the border
- the margin

The dimensions of a block are the sum of those of these four components.

This is something to keep in mind when building the design of your web pages.

THE PADDING

In CSS, the concept of **padding** refers to the "inner margin" that separates the content away from the edges of a block. The property we will use is padding and it takes a standard length value, either relative or absolute. Here is how it works.

```
p { padding: 35px; }
```

You can see the effect more clearly if you add a border and/or a background color to your elements.

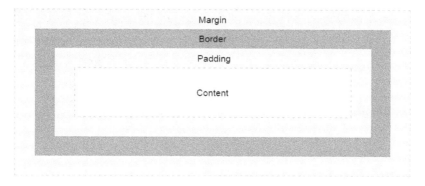

The padding in CSS

The should notice a 35 pixel padding around your paragraph, between the content itself and the border if there is any.

But there is a padding on all sides! I just wanted one on the left and right.

Indeed, using the `padding` property will apply space to all four sides of the block. The reason is that `padding` is not just a CSS property but a super-property or shorthand property.

As we've already seen them quite a bit by now I won't be going into to much detail on how they work, but you should know that super-properties allow you to combine multiple CSS properties into a single one. The `padding` property we just saw is precisely that. It merges the following four properties into one:

- `padding-top` : the padding on top of the element
- `padding-right` : the padding to the right of the element
- `padding-bottom` : the padding on the bottom of the element
- `padding-left` : the padding to the left of the element

Hence the following two codes producing the same result.

```
p { padding: 15px; }

p
{
    padding-top: 15px;
    padding-left: 15px;
    padding-bottom: 15px;
    padding-right: 15px;
}
```

The values for the padding of each different side don't need to be the same either. You could just as well enter four separate values. This is the order in which the values of each side should be specified.

```
padding: <top> <right> <bottom> <left>;
```

When dealing with shorthand properties and especially with value different geometrical points or sides in CSS, remember that the order is always a clockwise rotation starting from the top. As with the `border-radius` property that we introduced a while back, there are other ways to entered the values of each side with `padding`. You can for instance define only two values: the first for the top and bottom, the second for right and left. Or you can just write a single value and it will be applied to every side, which is what we've been doing until now. The figure below details these cases in more detail.

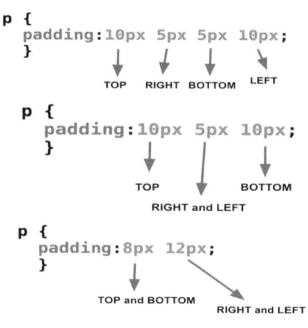

Differents ways to add padding in CSS

Whichever format you may need, always remember the order: clockwise and starting from the top.

THE MARGIN

What we call **margin** in CSS is the outer margin which separates the entire block, including any borders, from other elements outside of it. The property to do so is naturally called `margin`. It's used much in the same way as `padding` so we won't go through every single one of its applications. For example, if you waned to add a 35 pixel outer margin to your paragraphs you would write the following.

```
p { margin: 35px; }
```

Margins are used separate each element from one another as shown below.

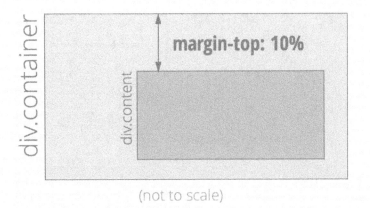

The margin in CSS

272

If you only need to add margins to a specific side you can use one of the following properties.

- `margin-top` : the margin on top of the element
- `margin-right` : the margin to the right of the element
- `margin-bottom` : the margin on the bottom of the element
- `margin-left` : the margin to the left of the element

You can also use the abridged form of the shorthand property.

```
margin: <top> <right> <bottom> <left>;
```

A few examples.

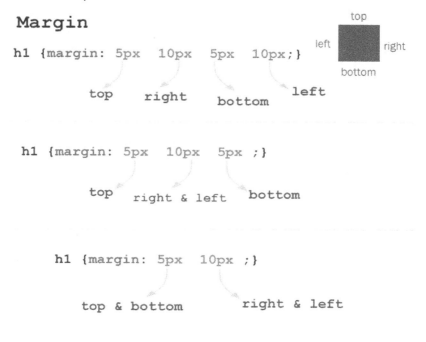

The margin in CSS

You should be familiar with this method by now, it works in the exact same way as with padding. The order is always the same: clockwise and starting from the top (top, right, bottom, left). You now know everything you need about CSS box models.

- Each HTML element can be represented by a box.
- These boxes all have dimensions.
- The dimensions of one box are the sum of those of its element's content, padding, borders and margins.

A quick test to evaluate your knowledge. Have a look at the following code.

```
p
{
    width: 500px;
    padding: 25px;
    border: 3px solid red;
    margin: 20px;
}
```

With what you've learned during this chapter, you should be able to tell me the exact value of the horizontal length of each box wrapping around the paragraphs. Hopefully you didn't answer 500 pixel. If you said 548 pixels, you're getting close but you're still retarded. The correct answer was of course **596 pixels** wide. Remember that by default most properties apply to all sides, that includes left AND right. It's easy to verify. We know that a CSS box is the composed of four parts: the content, the padding, the border and the margin.

Component	Width
Content	500 pixels
Padding	(25 * 2) = 50 pixels
Border	(3 * 2) = 6 pixels
Margin	(20 * 2) = 40 pixels
Total	**596 pixels**

A FEW MORE PROPERTIES

You thought this chapter was over? Admit it, you always fall for it. Technically we've covered the essentials of the CSS box model and you should be by now more than accustomed to how they work. But there are still a few noteworthy cases that warrant more explanations.

SWITCHING BETWEEN BLOCK AND INLINE

You might wonder how you can render an inline element as a block or vice-versa. As I mentioned previously, whether an element is inline or block is nothing more than default CSS behavior. It can be easily modified and whichever value you specify will override the default level type.

The property you need is `display` and its value is the type of rendering box you want for your element. For example, you can make your paragraphs inline and turn your links into blocks.

```
p { display: inline; }

a { display: block; }
```

What's the point, you may ask. In this particular instance there really isn't any. The default CSS rendering behavior was chosen for a reason, and it makes much more sense to have block paragraphs and inline links. But the `display` property is nonetheless very important in CSS. In addition to `block` and `inline`, and many other rendering box types, it can also take the value `none` to turn the element invisible. This is convenient if you need to make an element dynamically appear for example when the user clicks on a checkbox.

```
p { display: none; }
```

The above code will make your paragraphs invisible to the user, although they will still show up in the source code.

CENTERING A BLOCK

You may want to have a block centered either to the rest of the web page or in relation to another element.

The method for doing so is the same, and we won't even need to learn any new property. You only need two properties that we already learned about in this chapter.

- width : to specify the width of the element
- margin : to align the element to the center by setting the value to auto

When applied to the margin property, the auto value will provide automatic outer margins to the block. In practice that will enable you to center your element horizontally. For example.

```
p
{
    width: 300px;
    margin: auto;
}
```

This should give you a result that looks something like this.

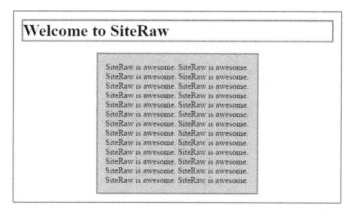

A centered block with CSS

If an item is nested within another element, it will of course be centered in relation to that element and not the rest of the HTML page.

Box sizing

Remember when I said that dimensions in CSS were additive rather than subtractive?

Keep that in mind and we'll come back to it in a moment. Since the dawn of CSS web designing, the box model has always worked as follows.

- **visible box**: content + padding + border
- **total box**: content + padding + border + margin

This can be a little counter-intuitive for beginners, as to determine the dimensions of the block rendered on screen you would have to add those of the content, the padding and the border while keeping in mind the the total allocated size would also include the outer margin.

See the following figure for a demonstration.

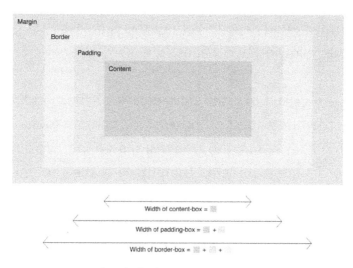

The default CSS box model

But what if I told you there was a way to make the total dimensions subtractive instead? This would simplify the box model considerably. Rather than adding the dimensions of the padding and border to those of the content, you would simply subtract them. This practice is considered a form of **box sizing**. Here is an example.

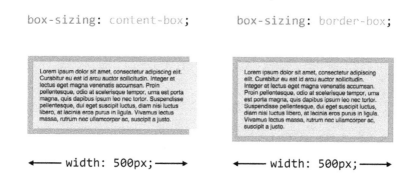

Box sizing with CSS

279

The property you need to achieve this is box-sizing. It can take the following two values.

- content-box : the dimensions of the padding and border are added to those of the content (default)
- border-box : the dimensions of the padding and border are subtracted from those of the content

Keep in mind that in both cases the dimensions of the outer margin are added to the total size of the box. A simple demonstration with one of our previous examples.

```
p
{
    width: 500px;
    padding: 25px;
    border: 3px solid red;
    margin: 20px;
}
```

We already calculated the total size of the visible box which was 556 pixels wide (596 pixels if you count the margins). But let's see what happens when we prepend and modify the box-sizing property.

```
p
{
    box-sizing: border-box;

    width: 500px;
    padding: 25px;
    border: 3px solid red;
    margin: 20px;
}
```

Now the total width of the visible box is only... 500 pixels (540 pixels if you count the outer margin). How is that possible? Because the width of the borders (3 + 3 = 6 pixels) and that of the padding (25 + 25 = 50 pixels) were subtracted, not added, to the width of the content. Which means that the final value of the width property was automatically altered to be no longer 500 pixels, but 444 pixels (500 - 50 - 6).

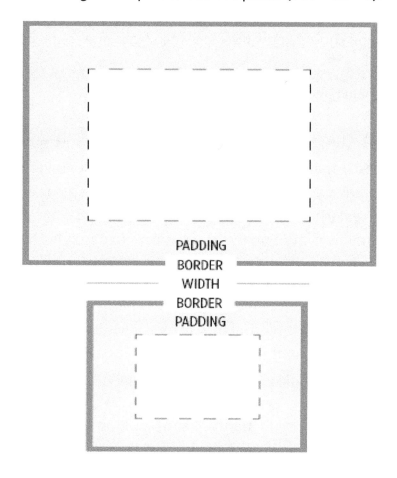

PADDING
BORDER
WIDTH
BORDER
PADDING

Default vs box sizing

As you can see from the figure above, the two methods will produce different results based nearly identical code.

 Which method should I use?

It's once again a matter of preference. The first method is more common simply by virtue of being the default option, but you should know how to switch from one to the other.

OVERFLOWING CONTENT

When working with absolute dimensions such as pixels or inches, it may happen that the content overflows vertically or sometimes even horizontally. The CSS property overflow was created specifically to check for overflowing content and determine what to do if such case were to occur. It can take the following values which affect the CSS behavior in case of an overflow.

- `visible` : the content will remain visible even outside the block limits (default)
- `hidden` : the content will be clipped outside of the block limits
- `scroll` : scroll bars will appear along the height and width of the content ensuring it doesn't overflow
- `auto` : similar to above only the scroll bars will only be displayed if necessary (if the content overflows)

To give you a visual example.

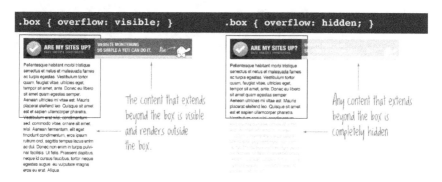

Overflow in CSS

Obviously none of these solutions are ideal, so it's always best to make sure that your content fits in the boundaries of the box or that you use relative dimensions.

OUTLINES

Finally, the CSS property outline allows you to add a "border" outside of both the padding and the actual border. It's a shorthand property that works almost exactly like border. You will certainly recognize the following syntax.

```
p { outline: <width> <style> <color>; }
```

For example.

```
p { border: 2px dashed black; outline: 5px
solid red; }
```

The following figure shows what outlines look like in CSS.

Outlines in CSS

If you don't want the outline glued to the border you can also use the property `outline-offset` to indicate a distance between the outline and the edge of the element.

```
p
{
    border: 2px dashed black;
    outline: 5px solid red;
    outline-offset: 20px;
}
```

I said outline worked almost like `border`, and it's true except for three minor differences.

- It always applies to all sides of an element (there is no ~~outline-right~~ for example)
- It isn't affected by `border-radius` or other CSS properties altering border styles
- Unlike borders, outlines aren't considered part of the box model so they don't change the dimensions of the element of adjacent elements

So what's their purpose?

Other than having cool double borders? It depends.

Outlines are often used to dynamically emphasize an element without affecting its positioning.

For example, adding a border upon a :hover might shift the element to one side or another if the horizontal dimensions of the border are asymmetrical.

Outlines on the other hand aren't dependent upon the box model, thus the element will remain in its original place.

FLEXBOX LAYOUTS

In the last two chapters we saw how to build the basic structure of our pages in HTML and how to manage the dimensions of our elements with CSS. It's time for the long awaited moment: when we learn all about CSS layouts. In other words we'll see how to change the position of the items on our web page, align certain elements and choose precisely where each and every block will appear. This is the final piece of the puzzle that we allow us to build actual websites that look like something. And the name of this piece is Flexbox... remember that name because we'll be using it often during this chapter. In fact, we might as well start out with an introduction to Flexbox. We'll cover where it began, why it was invented and especially what role it fills in web designing and web development. And don't worry... the practice will come soon enough.

INTRODUCTION TO FLEXBOX

Before we start introducing every Flexbox property, and trust me there are many, let's give a little introduction to the Flexbox model. We will first go over the history of Flexbox after which we will introduce the basic theory behind its operation.

A HISTORY OF FLEXBOX

Flexbox stands for Flexible Boxes and is a relatively new addition to the world of web designing.

The flexbox model

Prior to Flexbox, designing the layout of web pages in CSS was a notoriously intricate matter.

Here are a few of the ways web developers attempted to address this issue, in somewhat chronological order.

- At first, websites were designed using **HTML tables**. This predates even the CSS language and is considered severely obsolete (0/10 wnb).
- Then CSS appeared and we started building website layouts using the **float** property (5/10).
- Another method was to create **inline-block** elements which had their own specific attributes. This was only a marginal improvement over the float method and it came with its own set of drawbacks (5.5/10).
- Finally, since CSS3, we can now use the **Flexbox model**. How good is it? Keep reading.

Each successive method was conceived as an answer to the limitations of its predecessors. Flexbox was specifically designed to be flexible, as its name implies, but also to accommodate to the challenges of modern web development: integration with Javascript and other client-side languages, support of various screen resolutions and rendering devices and so on. The use of Flexbox ensures that elements behave in a predictable manner even when the page layout must accommodate to different screen sizes and display devices.

THE FLEXBOX MODEL

So the question you're probably asking yourselves right now

is: how does Flexbox work?

 How does Flexbox work?

The principle behind Flexbox layouts is remarkably simple: you define a container in which you place your elements. A container which holds one or more nested items. As long as you remember that rule you already know 99% of what there is to learn about Flexbox. You can also define multiple containers one after the other on the same web page, it will be up to you to create as many as necessary to get the layout you want. Let us begin by studying the behavior of a container.

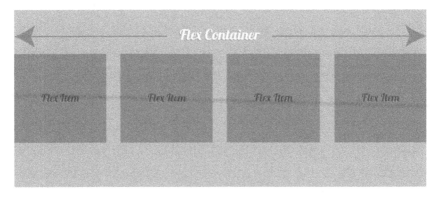

A flexbox container

Your Flexbox containers (and items) can be anything as long as they are block-level HTML elements. In one of our previous example, we used the <section> tag as a container for both the <article> and <aside> items.

You probably remember the following code excerpt.

```
<section>
    <article> [...] </article>

    <aside> [...] </aside>
</section>
```

But we can also use a more general example with <div> tags.

```
<div id="container">
    <div class="item">Item 1</div>

    <div class="item">Item 2</div>

    <div class="item">Item 3</div>
</div>
```

The container and items are respectively distinguished by the ID and class attributes.

 I already know that! The blocks will simply be placed one underneath the other.

True.

Since these are block elements they will follow the typical rules of the CSS box model that we saw in the previous chapter.

Let's add some colors to the items to see how they are organized.

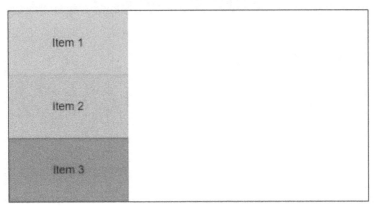

Default block positioning

Nothing new so far, this is the normal behavior of blocks. But what if we want to modify this behavior? That is the entire purpose of the Flexbox model.

ELEMENT DIRECTION

That was simply the theory, now let's discover the practical applications of Flexbox starting with the direction of the flow of these elements. But before that we need to define our Flexbox container. To do so you must add a single property to whichever element you want as your container, the `display` property. We already know a few of the values it can take such as `block` or `inline`, so let's introduce a new one... `flex`.

Here is the CSS code we are working with.

```
#container { display: flex; }
```

With this simple adjustment, our blocks are now placed side by side by default.

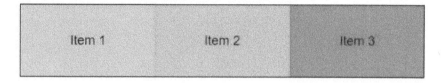

Flexbox block positioning

There are of course many more ways to handle the direction in which the elements are placed.

ELEMENT DIRECTION

Flexbox allows us to organize nested elements in the desired direction. The property for doing so is `flex-direction`, it's once again applied to the container and affects all child items. Here are the values it can take.

- `row` : organized on a row (default)
- `column` : organized on a column
- `row-reverse` : organized on a row in reverse order
- `column-reverse` : organized on a column in reverse order

Let's try appending our example with this new property.

293

```
#container
{
    display: flex;
    flex-direction: row-reverse;
}
```

And the result.

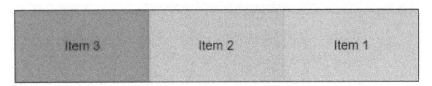

Flexbox reverse item order

You can see the difference: the blocks are now in reverse order. The HTML code remains identical, only the `flex-direction` property was added to the CSS code. You can apply any of the indicated values to this property. Below is a visual example of their effects.

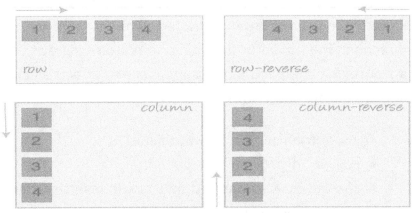

Flexbox direction illustration

Keep in mind that row *and* row-reverse *depend on the writing mode so in right-to-left context they will be reversed respectively.*

HANDLING THE WRAP

By default, blocks inside a container will try to stay on the same horizontal line which can lead to content overflowing and other graphical inconveniences. Flexbox somewhat solves this problem by dynamically reducing the width of each item should their combined dimensions exceed the maximum space available.

But you can also define the way you want the elements to wrap with the flex-wrap property.

Here are the values it can take.

- nowrap : all flex items will be laid out in a single line (default)
- wrap : in case of overflow the items will wrap onto multiple lines from top to bottom
- wrap-reverse : flex items will wrap onto multiple lines from bottom to top

Here is a visual illustration of this property.

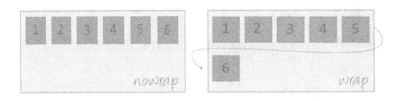

Flex-Wrap

Flexbox wrap demonstration

Going back to our example, we could add the following line of code.

```
#container
{
    display: flex;
    flex-direction: row-reverse;
    flex-wrap: wrap;
}
```

This would force a line-break in case of item overflow.

 For purposes of brevity, you can use the flex-flow shorthand property which combines the values of both flex-direction and flex-wrap. Its syntax is flex-flow: <direction> <wrap>.

FLEXIBLE ALIGNMENT

Let's review a bit of what we know. Items are organized either horizontally, by default, or vertically. This defines what is called the main axis. There is also a secondary axis (cross axis) perpendicular to the main axis.

- If your elements are organized horizontally, the cross axis is vertical
- If your elements are organized vertically, the cross axis is horizontal

Why am I telling you this? Because we're about to learn how to align our elements both on the main and secondary axes.

ALIGNMENT ON THE MAIN AXIS

We'll start with the simplest illustration, when elements are aligned horizontally (by default). The property we need to change their alignment is `justify-content`.

It can take these values.

- `flex-start` : items are packed toward the start line (default)
- `flex-end` : items are packed toward to end line
- `center` : items are aligned at the center of the container

- space-between : items are aligned with equal spacing between them
- space-around : same as above except they leave a natural padding space at their extremities

We can add this property to our demonstration code.

```
#container
{
    display: flex;
    justify-content: space-between;
}
```

But the best is still to test all possible values and see the results. See the figure below for a visual demonstration of these values.

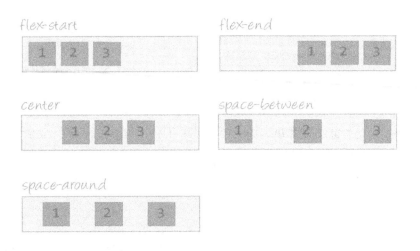

Flexbox justify content illustration

You see how the elements are aligned differently in each

different case? With a simple property, we can intelligently arrange our elements the way we want. It also works if your elements are in a vertical direction. In this case, the vertical axis becomes the main axis and justify-content functions much in the same fashion.

```
#container
{
    display: flex;
    flex-direction: column;
    justify-content: space-between;
}
```

Try it out and see the results for yourself.

ALIGNMENT ON THE SECONDARY AXIS

If our elements are placed in a horizontal direction (row), the secondary axis or cross axis is vertical. And conversely if our elements are in a vertical direction (column), the secondary axis is horizontal. To modify the alignment along the cross axis the property we need is align-items. It works very much like justify-content but in the perpendicular direction. Here are the values the align-items property can take.

- stretch: items are stretched over the entire axis (default)
- flex-start: items are stacked toward the start of the container
- flex-end: items are stacked toward the end of the container
- center: items are stacked to the center of the container
- baseline: items are stacked such that their baselines align

You can see case by case illustrations in the figure below.

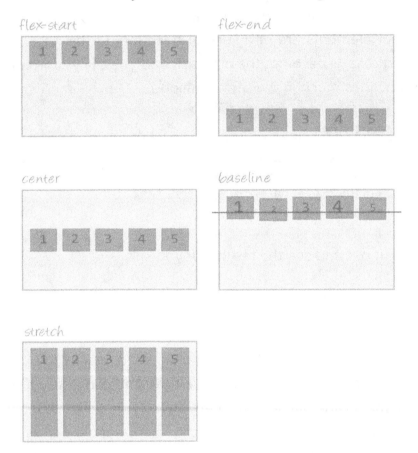

Flexbox align items illustration

In these examples we assume that our elements are in a horizontal direction but it works just as well vertically. And this concludes our work with the Flexbox model. Everything we learned in this chapter, and the two anterior ones, will be useful for what we're about to do next.

BUILDING YOUR WEBSITE

We're finally about to talk serious business. This is a rather special chapter, quite different from what you have read so far. Until now we've learned how to build basic web pages: adding content, organizing it with HTML and decorating it with CSS. Now we're about to put all that theory to practice: we're going to **create our first complete website**, from A to Z. Creating a website is not an easy task: you must be creative (like me), proficient (as myself) and talented (clearly, you've knocked on the right door). With that said, you have all the tools you need to start building a professional looking website. Let's get started.

CREATING THE BLUEPRINT

You're probably already thinking about how awesome your website is going to be. You're imagining the header, the menus, the background and all the great content you'll add.

And here's where I have to stop you. Not so fast. Before starting anything of the sort you first need to take a (mental) notepad and start designing the blueprint of your website. It doesn't need to be very elaborate, in fact it should be the most broad and concise possible, but you should nonetheless have a clear mental picture of what you're website will look like once completed. The bigger the project, the more valuable this blueprint becomes. Most of the time a simple scope statement and a few general guidelines are more than sufficient. Since this is presumably your first project of the sort I'll even help you out by giving you a theme: the exaltation of SiteRaw's awesomeness. A true Internet monument of worship to let people know just how extraordinary SiteRaw is. Here is the final result we will achieve at the end of this chapter.

A basic website

I intentionally went for the most simple and minimalist design possible, so as to put emphasis on the distinct elements that compose a website. We will also see how to create more advanced designs, with images, gradients and even more dynamic elements. For example, this is a slightly more advanced design variation that we will also cover in this chapter.

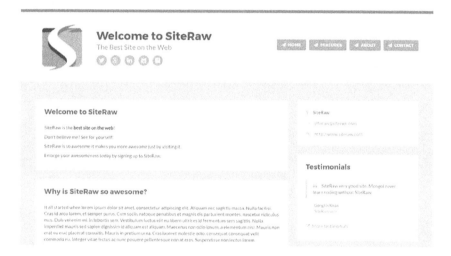

An intermediate website

So where do we start?

We know that a website is a combination of:

- Several HTML files which define the content of each page.
- One or more CSS files which specify the style and presentation of the site.

This is the order we will follow for this chapter. Structurally, it makes sense to start with HTML. You can have content without style but not the opposite. Let's get started!

ORGANIZING THE CONTENT

The first step is to lay the foundation of our HTML page. To do so we will re-use the basic code that we saw in some of the very first chapters of this tutorial.

```
<!DOCTYPE html>
<html>
    <head>
        <meta charset="utf-8" />
        <title>SiteRaw</title>
        <link rel="stylesheet" href="style.css" />
    </head>

    <body>

        <!-- Content -->

    </body>
</html>
```

The <head> portion is relatively complete so we won't be adding anything new. As we already know, the displayed content goes inside the <body> tag. So what do we write? I suggest you start with the HTML structural tags that we discovered at the beginning of this third part.

These will define the basic sections of each web page: the header, the menu, the footer and so on.

```html
<!DOCTYPE html>
<html>
    <head>
        <meta charset="utf-8" />
        <title>SiteRaw</title>
        <link rel="stylesheet" href="style.css" />
    </head>

    <body>

      <header>
            <!-- Header -->
      </header>

      <nav>
          <!-- Menu -->
      </nav>

      <section>
          <!-- Main Content -->
      </section>

      <footer>
          <!-- Footer -->
      </footer>

    </body>
</html>
```

You can recognize the four sections that shape most web pages: the header, the menu, the main content area and the footer. They are nearly universal in their application. This is just a template, there are of course other ways of breaking down the structure. But what do we place in each element?

THE HEADER

Headers are usually composed of either the title of the site, the logo, a banner or a combination thereof. To keep things as simple and straightforward as possible, I'll just use an <h1> title with an <h2> slogan or subtitle.

```
<header>
    <h1>Welcome to SiteRaw</h1>
    <h2>The Best Site on the Web</h2>
</header>
```

If you do want to use images, know that there are two ways to do so.

- You can use the <img /> tag that we saw in the first part of this tutorial.
- You can also add a background-image with CSS.

The second method is usually preferred for designing web layouts, as it allows you to dynamically alter the size, scale, position and even content of the image directly within the CSS file.

THE MENU

The menu or navigation bar will contain to essential browsing links that allow the user to go from one page to another.

Depending on what type of site you choose to build, and this is really up to you, the navigation menu you obtain will be quite different from mine. For my example I'll simply use the most general / all-purpose site structure.

```html
<nav>
  <ul>
    <li><a href="index.html">Home</a></li>
    <li><a href="features.html">Features</a></li>
    <li><a href="about.html">About</a></li>
    <li><a href="contact.html">Contact</a></li>
  </ul>
</nav>
```

You can place as many links as you want, just make sure that the navigation menu is consistent on all web pages.

THE MAIN SECTION

Unlike the header, menu and footer, the main section is a dynamic content area. This means that the content placed in this block will usually vary from page to page, in contrast to the other zones which remain fairly identical on all pages of your site.

We'll divide our main content area into two sections represented by the two HTML elements <article> and <aside>.

```
<section>
    <article>
        <!-- Content -->
    </article>

    <aside>
        <!-- Aside -->
    </aside>
</section>
```

So what do we put inside these elements? That is entirely up to you. Presumably, since every page will be different, you'll want separate content on each one: a brief introduction for the homepage, an in-depth description for the about page, a contact form for the contact page... We'll learn how to do that in subsequent chapters. For now I suggest just focusing on the homepage. You can add anything you want: titles, text content, images. An example is provided at the end of this part.

THE FOOTER

The footer is, as explained previously in this tutorial, the area in which you'll be placing content such as legal notices, contact information and so on. It's probably not the most interesting section of a website and doesn't really offer you much to express your creative freedom, so I suggest you simply add a typical copyright notice or whatever else of the same stripe.

Here is my example.

```
<footer>
    <p>© SiteRaw - <a href="http://www.siteraw.
com">www.siteraw.com</a> - The Best Site on the
Web.</p>
</footer>
```

Nothing very original, just a simple copyright notice and a repeat of the site subtitle.

THE COMPLETE HTML CODE

Now that we've added content to all four main blocks of our website, it's time to assemble every component into the final HTML site structure. Here is the complete HTML code.

```
<!DOCTYPE html>
<html>
    <head>
        <meta charset="utf-8" />
        <title>SiteRaw</title>
        <link rel="stylesheet" href="style.css" />
    </head>

    <body>
        <header>
            <h1>Welcome to SiteRaw</h1>
            <h2>The Best Site on the Web</h2>
        </header>

        <nav>
            <ul>
                <li><a href="index.
html">Home</a></li>
                <li><a href="features.
html">Features</a></li>
                <li><a href="about.
html">About</a></li>
```

```
        <li><a href="contact.
html">Contact</a></li>
      </ul>
    </nav>

    <section>
      <article>
        <h1>Welcome to SiteRaw</h1>

        <p>SiteRaw is the <strong>best
site on the web</strong>!</p>
        <p>Don't believe me? See for
yourself!</p>
        <p>SiteRaw is so awesome it
awesomizes you.</p>
        <p>Enlarge your awesomeness
today by signing up to SiteRaw.</p>

        <h2>Why is SiteRaw so
awesome?</h2>

        <p>It all started when lorem
ipsum dolor sit amet, consectetur adipiscing
elit. Aliquam nec sagittis massa. Nulla
facilisi. Cras id arcu lorem, et semper purus.
Cum sociis natoque penatibus et magnis dis
parturient montes, nascetur ridiculus mus.
[...]. Suspendisse non lectus lorem.</p>
      </article>

    <aside>
      <div class="aside">
        <h1>About SiteRaw</h1>

        <p>SiteRaw was founded
by God.</p>
      </div>

      <div class="aside">
        <h1>Testimonials</h1>

        <blockquote>SiteRaw very
good site. Mongol never learn coding without
```

```
SiteRaw.</blockquote>
                        <p class="name">Genghis
Khan</p>
                </div>
            </aside>
        </section>

        <footer>
            <p>© SiteRaw - <a href="http://www.
siteraw.com">www.siteraw.com</a> - The Best
Site on the Web.</p>
        </footer>

    </body>
</html>
```

Congratulations, you've built your first HTML page. While it certainly looks impressive at first glance keep in mind that there is are no novelties in this HTML code: you already know the purpose of every HTML tag we used. But we're not done with our website just yet. This is only the HTML portion, and only HTML without CSS does not make for the most visually pleasing experience ever. See for yourself...

HTML only website

WTF??? That's what I've been working on for an hour?? It sucks!!!

I know, I know... That's why I said we're not done yet. What's interesting is that this HTML code is more than enough for building any type of layout you want by adding CSS. We will see several examples of web designs further on in this chapter and they all use the same baseline HTML code.

FORMATTING THE DESIGN

Now that we have our HTML code handled, it's time to move onto the CSS. CSS is a very important part of any website as pretty much every line of code will have an influence on the final design. We will use most of the CSS property we have already seen in previous chapters, so in case you forgot what one of them does you can always go back to the chapter in which it was introduced. Or, if you're really lazy, you can just edit the values and see what happens. Let's start design our website.

CENTERING THE DESIGN

If you look back at the mockup of our design, you will notice that the main elements (header, navigation bar, menu and article content) are all centered horizontally. This is very easy to do in CSS, as we saw in the CSS box model chapter. All you need is to indicate a fixed width and set the margin property to auto. To makes things simple we will apply that property to the <body> tag, but you can of course create a new element specifically to serve as a container for the rest of your (centered) HTML elements. Here is the CSS code we will be using.

```css
html {
    background: #61905c;
    border-top: 10px solid #386b32;
    color: #fff;
    text-shadow: 2px 2px 0 rgba(0, 0, 0, 0.2);
}

body {
    width: 760px;
    margin: auto;
    padding: 20px;
    font: 14px arial;
}
```

You can already see the foundations of our design: the colors, the alignment of each component and the visual theme of the website. If you aren't satisfied with some of the design choices I make, feel free to modify the code until you get an adequate result. You might also have noticed that this code excerpt applies CSS rules to two HTML elements: <html> and <body>. While the latter is self-explanatory, indicating a fixed width and horizontally aligning the content to the center of the page, I didn't mention why I chose to apply other properties to the former.

This is because, in CSS, many styles affecting a parent element are inherited by their children. The parent element is the one containing other nodes or nested elements, which in turn are called children elements. If you want a visual demonstration of this concept, look at the following figure.

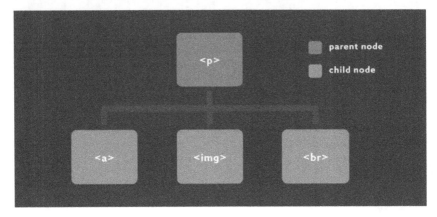

CSS inheritance structure

For instance, by applying a color property to the <html> tag, every element contained within that tag - meaning all of them since <html> is the root element - will inherit the same color... unless this rule is overwritten elsewhere in the CSS file. You can try it yourself by changing the color of the headings (<h1>) or the paragraphs (<p>).

DEFINING THE GLOBAL STYLES

While designing your website using CSS, you will naturally come to make a distinction between global styles affecting every element of a certain type, for example every paragraph

<p>, and more specific styles, only being applied to an individual element and/or its nested children, for example every paragraph <p> within the <aside> element. It's customary to start will the more general styles at the top of the CSS file and move down as you get more and more specific, if anything for the sake of future readability. In our example we already defined a background color, a text color and even centered the elements. Those would be considered global styles or general styles. There are still a few more details we can add before moving on to modifying the layout of each individual element.

```css
a {
    color: #a6d8a5;
    text-decoration: none;
}

a:hover { text-decoration: underline; }

nav, article, .aside, footer {
    background: #407d38;
    padding: 0;
    box-shadow: 2px 2px 2px #386b32;
}

nav, footer {
    margin: 10px 0;
    padding: 0 15px;
}

footer {
    text-align: center;
    padding: 10px 0;
}
```

In this code we added a background to each main component of our website (navigation bar, article, aside, footer) and we made our links a little more visually pleasing - the default blue/ purple on a green background isn't the most aesthetically pleasing.

HEADER AND NAVIGATION

Now that the general layout of our site is handled, we can move on to designing the more intricate parts. Let's start with the header and navigation menu. The header of our website is comprised of two heading titles, <h1> and <h2>. Since the header is intended to be one of the most striking aspect of a website's visual identity, we can't really leave those two headings with the default layout. Here is a simple CSS code we can use to improve them a bit.

```
header h1 {
    font: 25px/19px Impact;
    letter-spacing: 2px;
    margin-bottom: 0;
    font-weight: 300;
    text-transform: uppercase;
}

header h2 {
    font: 15px "Comic Sans MS";
    font-weight: 300;
}
```

You can use any of the properties we've seen thus far, you can even choose to replace the headings with a logo or a banner if you want.

316

For the navigation menu, since we want a horizontal menu rather than the default vertical bullet list, we have to change the display type of each individual bullet from block to inline. Other than that, there isn't much difficulty in this code.

```
nav ul {
    padding: 0;
    text-align: center;
}

nav ul li {
    display: inline;
    padding: 0 50px;
    line-height: 40px;
}
```

Those two CSS rules sets are enough to give you a horizontal menu and make it fit the layout of your website. As always, you can edit the properties as needed.

THE COMPLETE CSS CODE

Just as I did with the HTML, I'll give you my version of the CSS code.

The result should be similar to what I showed at the beginning of this chapter, though if you edited my examples along the way - which I recommend - yours results will obviously differ from mine.

Here is the complete CSS code.

```css
html {
    background: #61905c;
    border-top: 10px solid #386b32;
    color: #fff;
    text-shadow: 2px 2px 0 rgba(0, 0, 0, 0.2);
}

body {
    width: 760px;
    margin: auto;
    padding: 20px;
    font: 14px arial;
}

nav {
    border-bottom: 4px solid #47873d;
    height: 40px;
}

nav, article, .aside, footer {
    background: #407d38;
    padding: 0;
    box-shadow: 2px 2px 2px #386b32;
}

nav, footer {
    margin: 10px 0;
    padding: 0 15px;
}

a {
    color: #a6d8a5;
    text-decoration: none;
}
a:hover { text-decoration: underline; }

header h1 {
    font: 25px/19px Impact;
    letter-spacing: 2px;
    margin-bottom: 0;
    font-weight: 300;
    text-transform: uppercase;
}
```

```css
header h2 {
    font: 15px "Comic Sans MS";
    font-weight: 300;
}

nav ul {
    padding: 0;
    text-align: center;
}

nav ul li {
    display: inline;
    padding: 0 50px;
    line-height: 40px;
}

section {
    display: flex;
    justify-content: space-between;
}

article {
    flex: 0 0 530px;
    margin-right: 10px;
    text-align: justify;
}

article p { padding: 0 30px; }

article h1, article h2 {
    margin: 25px 50px 21px 0;
    padding-left: 20px;
    background: #335f2e;
    font: bold 15px/30px Helvetica;
    box-shadow: 0 2px 0 #234f1e;
}

.aside {
    padding-bottom: 5px;
    margin-bottom: 20px;
}
```

```css
aside h1 {
    margin: 0 0 20px;
    text-align: center;
    background: #335f2e;
    font: bold 14px/27px Helvetica;
    box-shadow: 0 1px 0 #234f1e;
}

aside p {
    padding: 0 15px;
}

blockquote {
    font-style: italic;
    margin: 0 15px;
    color: #a6d8a5;
}

blockquote:before, blockquote:after {
    content: "\""; /* adds a quote before and
after */
    font-size: 25px;
}

footer {
    text-align: center;
    padding: 10px 0;
}
```

That was the last bit of CSS, and with this our design is finally finished.

You can see what it looks like one the next page.

The final result

Now that the design is finished, you know how to proceed, what are the guidelines to follow, and how you can make your own website layout from scratch. It's up to you to create a unique design for your site, to put your colors, your background images, your effects, your fonts. The sky is the limit. You are allowed, and invited, to use my CSS code as a model. I know that all these lines of code can make you feel dizzy at first, especially for beginners who have never built a website before. The good news is that with practice you will not only not feel dizzy at the sight of CSS code anymore, you will also be able to create an entire design without the help of anyone.

It might even be better than mine (non-contractual assertion - results may vary - I am a genius after all).

A COMPLETE WEBSITE

Now that we have both our HTML and CSS codes, what could possibly be left to cover? For starters, we only ever built one HTML page... a website is (hopefully) more than just one page. Adding more content to your website is easy, it's only a matter of creating new pages and linking them together. Don't forget to import the CSS file on all pages, so that they share the same design.

 What if I don't like the design? Does that mean I have to start over from scratch?

Yes and no. Remember that only the CSS code is involved in the customization of the design. Look at the HTML we wrote: there is no information about visual rendering, only about the content to be displayed. That's what I've been repeating since the beginning of this tutorial so hopefully you get it by now: HTML for the content, CSS for the presentation. By modifying the CSS you can change the entire layout of your website without touching any HTML code. Let's use a practical example to demonstrate.

For instance, if you don't like the design we used in our example and wanted something completely different, all you would need is to modify the CSS file. Here is a different version of the exact same website.

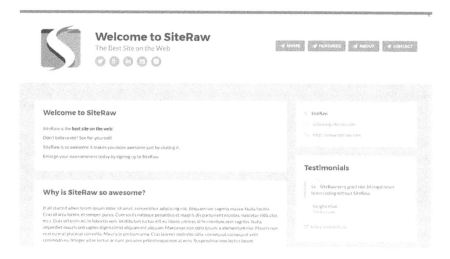

A different design

Same HTML, different CSS. Not satisfied? Let's try something else.

Another CSS web layout

Still not good enough? Let's try something a little more advanced.

A slightly more advanced website

Or you could go for something more minimalist and ergonomic. Always with the same HTML code.

A somewhat minimalist design

These "more advanced" designs are not necessarily more complex than what we've seen until now, but they do require more fine-tuning and therefore more CSS code. What style of design you pick depends on the type of website you are building. A My Little Pony themed fashy political tabloid might not be the best option. With this, we've finally built our first complete website.

What's left to learn in this tutorial? You'll find out in the next chapters.

PART IV

ADVANCED FEATURES

HTML TABLES

Now that we built our website (see the last chapters of the previous part), what could possibly be left to cover in this tutorial? This might come to a surprise to some of you, but we still aren't done with HTML and CSS. There are many more so-called "advanced", and I use this term loosely, features that we have yet to discover. Amongst them are tables. You probably know what a table is, defined as a set of facts or figures systematically displayed, usually in rows and columns. We'll start by introducing the concept of tables in HTML, particularly detailing their use, before building our own simple tables, then moving on to a slightly more complex variety, and finally concluding this chapter with a special case: when you need to merge either rows or columns. We'll see a bit of CSS too, but most of the properties we'll use have already been covered in previous chapters. Tables are easy, tables are fun, and my use of the "advanced" adjective was more out of terminological laziness than anything. There is nothing complicated about this HTML feature, so let's begin without further ado.

AN INTRODUCTION TO TABLES

Tables are a new way of organizing content in HTML. Imagine you want to make a list of every computer language you know of.

 We already know how to do that! All we need are the <ul> and <li> tags!

That's true. We saw in the Organize your text chapter how to create bullet lists. But imagine that in addition to showing the names of every computing language you know of, you also want to display their current version, the year in which they were invented and their purpose. We can try the following code.

```
<ul>
    <li>HTML (5, 1991, markup)</li>
    <li>CSS (3, 1996, presentation)</li>
    <li>Javascript (1, 1995, scripting)</li>
</ul>
```

This would give us the following result.

- HTML (5, 1991, markup)
- CSS (3, 1996, presentation)
- Javascript (1, 1995, scripting)

It gets the job done, but it's not very readable.

The problem with this example is that there is more than one value per list item.

We would need something that makes comparing each individual value easier and more ergonomic. Something with both rows and columns. Something like... tables. Here is an example of what you can obtain with tables in HTML and CSS.

Language	Version	Founded	Purpose
HTML	5	1991	Markup
CSS	3	1996	Presentation
Javascript	1	1995	Scripting

Much easier on the eyes. This is just a basic table with minimal CSS. If you want to see a more elaborate example of what is possible with tables, have a look at the figure below.

Tables in HTML and CSS

Pretty cool, right? Keep reading this chapter to see how you can achieve similar results, and much more. But before anything we should start with basics.

SIMPLE HTML TABLES

While tables are great for organizing information in a clear and readable way, their implementation on a web page is a bit more complex than what we are used to. The reason is that to display a table, you need to write a specific sequence of multiple nested HTML tags in the correct order. When you think about it, even the most basic tables are composed of at least four elements.

- a table container
- rows
- columns
- table cells

If you want to simplify things even further, you don't even need to define rows, columns and table cells, as knowing the numerical value of at least two of these variables allows you to determine the third without it being specified. We can safely remove one of those three variables. The creators of HTML must have thought that having a column tag would be redundant so... bye columns.

We are now left we three components: the container, the rows and the table cells. And it just so happens that the HTML language has a specific tag for each of these three elements.

- \<table> for the table
- \<tr> for the rows (stands for table row)
- \<td> for the cells (stands for table data cell)

Let's see what all these tags do, and how they are used in conjunction with one another.

THE CONTAINER ELEMENT

The first HTML element you need to know is the \<table> tag. This is the table container which, by definition, will contain everything else that we will cover in this chapter. It's a block tag, so it has to be placed outside of paragraphs.

```
<p>A paragraph before the table.</p>

<table>
    <!-- The table itself -->
</table>

<p>A paragraph after the table.</p>
```

Obviously, this code alone won't do much: it simply delineates the beginning and end of a table. To add content to our table we will need to use the two other tags we just discovered: \<tr> and \<td>.

333

TABLE ROWS AND DATA CELLS

As I said before, creating tables in HTML is simply a matter of placing these tags in the correct sequence. First we create our table rows with the <tr> element, then we add as many cells as we want inside each row with <td>.

For example, if I want a table with two rows and three columns per line, I can write the following.

```
<table>
    <tr>
        <td>HTML</td>
        <td>Markup</td>
        <td>1991</td>
    </tr>

    <tr>
        <td>CSS</td>
        <td>Presentation</td>
        <td>1996</td>
    </tr>

    <tr>
        <td>Javascript</td>
        <td>Scripting</td>
        <td>1995</td>
    </tr>
  <table>
```

Remember the order: table > row > cell.

You can obviously add as many rows and cells per line as you want.

HTML	Markup	1991
CSS	Presentation	1996
Javascript	Scripting	1995

A table illustration

 That sucks! It doesn't even look like a table!

That's because we haven't added any CSS yet.

STYLING TABLES WITH CSS

A plain HTML table isn't very aesthetically pleasing to say the least, so let's move on to the CSS for now. The first step would be to add a border to each cell like I did in my illustrations. We already know the property used to add borders to an element, all that's left is to apply it to the <td> tag. And for good measure, let's also add a padding and center the text horizontally.

```
td
{
    border: 1px solid #aaa;
    padding: 5px;
    text-align: center;
}
```

And the result.

HTML	Markup	1991
CSS	Presentation	1996
Javascript	Scripting	1995

Adding borders to our cells

You may have noticed that the borders which we have now made visible are separated via a margin by default. What if we want only a single border between each cell and no margin? Fortunately, there is a CSS property that applies only to tables and that does exactly that.

BORDER COLLAPSING

The border-collapse property is used to indicate whether a table's borders should be separated or collapsed.

It can take two values:

- separate : adjacent cells have distinct borders (default).
- collapse : adjacent cells have shared borders.

Since our goal is to have a single shared border, let's try to second value.

Don't forget that it applies to the table element.

```
table { border-collapse: collapse; }

td
{
    border: 1px solid #aaa;
    padding: 5px;
    text-align: center;
}
```

You can see the result below.

HTML	Markup	1991
CSS	Presentation	1996
Javascript	Scripting	1995

Adding borders to our cells

That looks much more like a table. You can of course use any other CSS property you know of to stylize either the table, the rows or the cells as much as you wish.

CSS table border styles

ADVANCED HTML TABLES

Up until now we've learned how to create tables as well as add rows and data cells. That's cool, but still pretty limited. Time to discover some more advanced features of HTML.

HEADER CELLS

Tables are a great way to display data in a readable and accessible fashion. But to be able to make sense and use of the data displayed, you need to understand what each column represents. In addition to the <td> element (table data cell), HTML also provides us with a <th> tag that stands for table header cell. The latter is used just like the former, except for the fact that it contains header content. Header content will generally be a description of the column containing the header cell. Expanding upon our demonstration table.

```
<table>
    <tr>
        <th>Name</th>
        <th>Purpose</th>
        <th>Founded</th>
    </tr>

    <tr><td>HTML</td><td>Markup</td><td>1991</td></tr>
    <tr><td>CSS</td><td>Presentation</td><td>1996</td></tr>
    <tr><td>Javascript</td><td>Scripting</td><td>1995</td></tr>

<table>
```

You can see the result in the figure below.

Name	Purpose	Founded
HTML	Markup	1991
CSS	Presentation	1996
Javascript	Scripting	1995

A table with header cells

By default the browser will display the header text in bold, but you can change it in CSS.

Remember that header cells <th> replace regular data cells <td>. For some reason, a lot of beginners get confused and replace the entire table row <tr> with <th>... header cells, not header rows.

THE SCOPE ATTRIBUTE

Not very often used but good to know nonetheless, <th> possesses an element specific attribute: scope. The scope attribute determines the cells that the header relates to.

It can take the following two values.

- col : the header relates to the column it belongs to (default).
- row : the header relates to the row it belongs to.

The only reason why you'd want a header relating to one of your rows is if you are using a double entry table or double entry matrix.

	1	2	3
1	1	2	3
2	2	4	6
3	3	6	9

A multiplication table

And here is the code to produce the above result.

```
<table>
    <tr>
        <th></th>
        <th scope="col">1</th>
        <th scope="col">2</th>
        <th scope="col">3</th>
    </tr>
```

```
    <tr><th scope="row">1</th><td>1</td><td>2</
td><td>3</td></tr>
    <tr><th scope="row">2</th><td>2</td><td>2</
td><td>6</td></tr>
    <tr><th scope="row">3</th><td>3</td><td>6</
td><td>9</td></tr>
</table>
```

You can use both header cells <th> and regular data cells <td> on the same row to produce a table with vertical headings. This isn't often used outside of double entry tables (what we just saw).

A TABLE CAPTION

We learned about header cells which describe the content of each column they belong to. It makes the table more readable. But we're still lacking something to explain the purpose of the table itself, not just that of the columns or rows.

Tables often have titles used to do just that: in our example, our title would be something like "*The languages of websites*".

The HTML element we need is called <caption> and it contains the title of your table.

Here is how it's used.

```
<table>
    <caption>Web languages</caption>

    <tr>
        <th>Name</th>
        <th>Purpose</th>
        <th>Founded</th>
    </tr>

    <tr><td>HTML</td><td>Markup</td><td>1991</
td></tr>

    <tr><td>CSS</td><td>Presentation</
td><td>1996</td></tr>

    <tr><td>Javascript</td><td>Scripting</
td><td>1995</td></tr>
<table>
```

You can see the result below.

Web languages

Name	Purpose	Founded
HTML	Markup	1991
CSS	Presentation	1996
Javascript	Scripting	1995

A table with a caption

We can apply CSS styles to the table caption just like any other HTML element.

STYLING THE CAPTION

You can change the caption position using the CSS caption-side property which applies to the caption element and can take the the following two values.

- top : the caption will be placed above the table (default).
- bottom : the caption will be placed below the table.

Let's add some CSS to our caption to make it stand out.

```
caption
{
    caption-side: bottom;
    font-weight: bold;
    letter-spacing: 1px;
    font-style: italic;
}
```

And the result.

Name	Purpose	Founded
HTML	Markup	1991
CSS	Presentation	1996
Javascript	Scripting	1995
Web languages		

A caption with CSS

The two CSS properties border-collapse and caption-side are noteworthy as they are specific to tables, so you won't run into them very often. They are also the only two new CSS properties we will cover in this chapter.

STRUCTURED TABLES

We could leave our table like this. But if you want your tables to be even more semantically structured, you may want to divide them into several distinct fields. HTML has three elements, one for each table part.

- <thead> : for the heading of the table
- <tbody> : for the body of the table
- <tfoot> : for the footer of the table

These new elements wrap around the table rows <tr>.

 What's the point of using another tag for the heading? Don't we already have <th> to do that?

The <th> element indicates that the table cell contains column header information, thus it replaces the "regular" data cell <td> element. It can be used either independently or in conjunction with <thead>. The <thead> element on the other hand specifies that the entire row, or set of rows, contained within are to be treated as headers.

The best way to understand the purpose of these three tags is to add them to our example, dividing our table into three distinct parts.

```
<table>
    <caption>Web languages</caption>

    <thead>
        <tr><th>Name</th><th>Purpose</
th><th>Founded</th></tr>
    </thead>

    <tfoot>
        <tr><th>Name</th><th>Purpose</
th><th>Founded</th></tr>
    </tfoot>

    <tbody>
        <tr><td>HTML</td><td>Markup</
td><td>1991</td></tr>

        <tr><td>CSS</td><td>Presentation</
td><td>1996</td></tr>

        <tr><td>Javascript</td><td>Scripting</
td><td>1995</td></tr>
    </tbody>
<table>
```

The order of elements is now `table > thead/tbody/ tfoot > tr > th/td`.

I added a bit of CSS to the result to delineate the three different fields of our table.

Name	Purpose	Founded
HTML	Markup	1991
CSS	Presentation	1996
Javascript	Scripting	1995
Name	Purpose	Founded
Web languages		

A semantically structured table

Something you might have noticed is that the table footer <tfoot> is above the <tbody> element in our HTML code. This is just a code convention, probably for practical accessibility reasons since the content within <tbody> usually takes up the most space.

 Why are the <thead> and <tfoot> lines identical?

In very long tables, where you might want to visitor to avoid having to scroll all the way back to the top to see what each column is about, it's common to simply duplicate the header cells. The footer can also be used to include otherwise important yet ancillary information, such as the sum total of each cell when dealing with numerical values. It's obviously not the case in our example, so I went with the first application.

 You don't necessarily need to use all three elements we learned about (<thead>, <tbody> and <tfoot>). I only recommend them for larger and more complex tables that need to be divided, for simple tables you can just skip them entirely. When none of these tags are present, the table is interpreted as if it consisted entirely of a <tbody> section.

MERGING TABLE CELLS

We learned how to build simple tables, complex tables and even how to stylize our cells using CSS. What could be left to cover in this chapter?

Merging cells.

Both header cells <th> and data cells <td> can be merged horizontally or vertically using either one, or both, of these HTML attributes.

- colspan : defines how many columns a cell can occupy
- rowspan : defines how many rows a cell can occupy

The default value of both these attributes is 1. If I wanted one of my tables cells to take up two "spaces" horizontally, I would write: <td colspan="2">. But the best way to understand how these attributes work is through a practical example.

Let's adjust our demonstration table into the following.

```
<table>
    <tr>
        <th></th>
        <th scope="col">Markup?</th>
        <th scope="col">Style?</th>
        <th scope="col">Awesome?</th>
    </tr>

    <tr><th scope="row">HTML</th><td>Yes<//
td><td>Deprecated</td><td>No</td></tr>

    <tr><th scope="row">CSS</th><td>No<//
td><td>Yes</td><td>No</td></tr>

    <tr><th scope="row">SiteRaw</th><td>No<//
td><td>No</td><td>Yes</td></tr>
</table>
```

You can see the result on the next page.

	Markup?	Style?	Awesome?
HTML	Yes	Deprecated	No
CSS	No	Yes	No
SiteRaw	No	No	Yes 😎

A regular table

As you can see, there are a few adjacent cells that contain the same information: the last cells of the first two rows and the first two cells of the last row. We can merge them together using the HTML attributes we just discovered.

```
<tr>
    <th>HTML</th>
    <td>Yes</td>
    <td>Deprecated</td>
    <td rowspan="2">No</td>
</tr>

<tr>
    <th>CSS</th>
    <td>No</td>
    <td>Yes</td>
</tr>

<tr>
    <th>SiteRaw</th>
    <td colspan="2">No</td>
    <td>Yes</td>
</tr>
```

I removed the scope attributes (they are optional) so you could see more clearly to which cells colspan and rowspan are applied. Here is the result.

	Markup?	Style?	Awesome?
HTML	Yes	Deprecated	No
CSS	No	Yes	
SiteRaw	No		Yes 😎

A table with merged cells

As you can see, two pairs of cells have been merged: horizontally on the bottom left and vertically on the top right. You aren't limited to merging only two cells, you can apply whatever value you want to these attributes provided it doesn't surpass the total number of available cells per line or column. You can also apply both attributes to the same cell if you ever need to (you won't).

When the value of either colspan or rowspan is greater than 1, meaning that the cell takes up more than its default allocated space, you have to manually adjust your table by removing the now duplicate cells on other lines or columns. In our code example, you can see that some row have "missing" cells.

You thought this chapter was over?

Think again! Allow me to introduce... multidimensional 4D tables!!! With HTML physical chairs and sheeit.

On second thought, that may be too advanced even for you.

Better move on to the next chapter.

FORMS

Any HTML page can be enhanced with interactive form that allow the visitor to fill in information, select an item amongst a menu of several available options and even click a button to send the data contained in your form to another page.

Forms are pretty much everywhere on the Internet so you might be wondering why we waited so long before introducing them. The reason is that we have reached what we can call a "limit" of the HTML and CSS languages.

At the beginning of this tutorial I said that HTML and CSS were sufficient for creating a website, and it's true. But I never said that you could do everything with them. HTML and CSS are markup and style sheet languages, respectively. They allow you to create web pages and design them as much as you want and, while they are web languages, they aren't stricto sensu programming languages.

We can create forms in HTML, we can stylize them in CSS, we can even send the data they contain to another page of our website... but we can't process that data without a server-side (back-end) programming language. By the end of this chapter you'll understand what I mean. But for now, let's start creating forms.

CREATING A FORM

Before creating our form elements we first have to define the form container itself, just as we did with tables in the previous chapter. The HTML element for delineating the start and end of a form is <form>. Here is how you use it.

```
<p>A paragraph before the form.</p>

<form>
    <!-- The form itself -->
</form>

<p>A paragraph after the form.</p>
```

Every form control we create will be contained inside the <form> element.

But before we can move on to the actual controls, there are two important attributes we should cover.

- `method` : the method by which the form data will be submitted
- `action` : the page to which the form data will be submitted

The `action` attribute is pretty self-explanatory: it's simply the target page to which the data entered in your forms will be sent, the current URI (page) by default. For `method` things get a little more complicated, as it defines the method by which the data will be sent.

FORM METHOD

There exist many types of HTTP requests: HEAD, GET, POST, PUT, etc. Only two are relevant to HTML forms: GET and POST. And it just so happens that `get` and `post` are the two values that can be taken by the `method` attribute. Let's see how these work.

THE GET METHOD

This is the default method for sending form data. Using the `get` method will send the data as URL variables, meaning it will append your page address with whatever information was entered in your form. Have you ever seen a web address (URL) looking something like this?

```
http://www.siteraw.com/?name1=value&name2=value
```

If so, chances are high you were dealing with a GET method of data transmission. This is perhaps the most straightforward method but it does have some inconveniences. The most evident being the fact that any data sent will be visible in the URL.

But this can also turn into an advantage since having visible data means the result page can be bookmarked and accessed directly without having to re-submit the form (e.g. `http://www.siteraw.com/search?q=html`).

THE POST METHOD

This is the preferred method for most types of forms. In this case, the form data will be appended to the body of the HTTP request, meaning that it will not be directly visible in the address bar. In addition and unlike with the GET method, there is no limit to the amount of data you can send. This is the method we will use.

SETTING UP THE FORM

We can now adjust our form using these two attributes. For the `method` attribute we will use the `post` value and for `action` we will simply enter `target.html`, a fictitious page to which the form data will be submitted. As I said, we can't actually process said data with HTML and CSS alone, so we'll just pretend the ~~Death Star~~ page is fully operational for now.

By the power of imagination. Here is our updated code.

```html
<p>A paragraph before the form.</p>

<form method="post" action="target.html">
    <!-- The form itself -->
</form>

<p>A paragraph after the form.</p>
```

Now that we've handled the form container, let's find out how to insert text fields, checkboxes, radio buttons and more.

Here is an example of what can be achieve using HTML and CSS.

A complete form using HTML and CSS

Want to learn how to do that? Then keep reading this chapter.

INPUT FIELDS

The most common form control element is input field. The HTML element we need is <input />, which is a standalone tag. Remember this tag well, as we'll be using it for 90% of all form related controls. Seriously. But having an <input /> tag alone isn't enough to produce a functional form control element. You also need to give it a type attribute. The form element will be different depending on the value it takes.

SINGLE-LINE TEXT FIELD

One-line text input fields allow the visitor to enter textual information on a single line. They are often used for names, usernames, ages or email addresses. You've certainly already seen them, but just in case I'll show you an example of something we can create with minimal HTML code.

Username : [   ]

A basic text input field

To create a single-line text input field, the value of the type property we want is text. We can add the following inside our form container.

```
<input type="text" />
```

You can try it out and see the result for yourself. But our text input field is not complete yet. The way forms work is that each input contains data that is sent, once the form is submitted, to a target page (here target.html). Each data segment is constituted of a pair: name and value. The value is whatever the visitor enters in the field while the name is an indicator of whatever the field is supposed to represent.

It just so happens that HTML allows us to use an attribute to specify that: the name attribute. And let's also add an id attribute, we'll see why in just a moment.

```
<input type="text" name="username"
id="username" />
```

You can use the same value for both name and id, it's not a problem.

LABELS

In HTML, labels are used as captions for items in a user interface. Why are they useful? We know that our text input field is for usernames, since we built it... but what about the actual visitor?

Shouldn't we have a way to tell him: this is the field for your username?

Luckily there is an HTML element for that: <label>. It's an inline tag that you can place before or after your input field, and it contains whatever explanatory text you want associated with your input.

```
<label>Username</label> : <input type="text"
name="username" id="username" />
```

But that isn't all labels do. You can also link the label to the input control, meaning that whenever the visitor clicks the label text he will be focused on the control. To do so you must add a for attribute to the <label> that matches the id attribute of the <input />. That's why we added an id above, in case you were wondering. Here is our completed code.

```
<form method="post" action="target.html">
  <p>

    <label for="username">Username</label> :

    <input type="text" name="username"
id="username" />

  </p>
</form>
```

This code will give you the exact result you saw in the previous illustration. Try clicking on the label to see the binding effect: your cursor should automatically be focused on the corresponding text field.

A FEW ADDITIONAL ATTRIBUTES

There are a few additional attributes that can be added to the <input /> element to further customize its operation.

- `minlength` : specifies the minimum number of characters the user can enter
- `maxlength` : specifies the maximum number of characters the user can enter (most browsers will prevent the user from typing more characters than the limit)
- `value` : pre-populates the field with a chosen value
- `placeholder` : somewhat similar to the above as it displays a default text inside the field, except this text isn't counted as the field's value and disappears as soon as the user focuses on the control

You can play around with these attributes to see how they work in greater detail.

PASSWORD FIELD

Password fields are somewhat similar to regular text fields, except that you can't see whatever characters you type into the control.

To create this type of field you just need to use the password value on your type attribute. There rest is pretty much identical to what we saw above.

```
<form method="post" action="target.html">
  <p>
    <label for="username">Username</
label> : <input type="text" name="username"
id="username" />
  </p>

  <p>
    <label for="password">Password</label>
 : <input type="password" name="password"
id="password" />
  </p>
</form>
```

You can see the result below.

Username : [   ]

Password : [●●●●●●●●●●●]

A password entry field

As you can see, the characters entered in the password field aren't shown on the screen.

MULTI-LINE TEXT FIELD

I said that 90% of form controls involved the <input /> tag. Multi-line text fields are an exception as we'll be using a new HTML element: <textarea>. We well be using the same attributes as with single-line entry fields, except for type which is unnecessary.

And just like the <input /> element, <textarea> can be linked with a <label> using the same mechanism. Let's see how it works.

```
<form method="post" action="target.html">
    <p><label for="siteraw">Describe the
awesomeness of SiteRaw in your own words.</
label></p>

    <p><textarea name="siteraw" id="siteraw"></
textarea></p>
</form>
```

And the result.

Describe the awesomeness of SiteRaw in your own words.

A textarea entry field

Just as with single-line inputs, you can add as much text as you want. The difference is that here you can hit the Enter key to produce line breaks.

You can also edit the height and width of the input field with CSS, which is what I did since the default dimensions are a bit small.

Why is there nothing inside the <textarea> tag? We just open it and close it immediately afterwards, wouldn't it have been simpler if it was a standalone tag?

That's because there is no `value` attribute for the <textarea> element. If you want to pre-populate the field with a default text, you just enter your content between the opening and the closing tag. See below.

```
<textarea name="siteraw" id="siteraw">Your
default text.</textarea>
```

And the result.

Describe the awesomeness of SiteRaw in your own words.

SiteRaw gave me colorectal cancer.

A textarea with default text

The other attributes we covered, such as `maxlength` and `placeholder`, are applicable to <textarea>. If you use CSS, you can try to match the style of both single-line and multi-line input fields.

ENHANCED ENTRY FIELDS

In HTML5 there are many new features available related to form entry fields. These are made available by modifying the type attribute of the <input /> element, just as we did for password fields. Here are some of these new form control features.

 Keep in mind that not all browsers will display these (relatively) new elements. But that's okay since even if the browser doesn't recognize a specific field it will show a regular single-line text input control instead.

SEARCH FIELD

Search fields are similar to regular text entry controls except for the fact that they are semantically marked as distinct form elements. To turn an input control into a search field, simply use the search value.

```
<input type="search" />
```

You won't see much difference with a regular text field... until you start writing.

Some browsers will then display a small cross to the right-side of the field, allowing you to quickly clear whatever you've typed in.

Text: SiteRaw

Search: SiteRaw   ✕

A search field

Other browsers will add a small magnifying glass to distinguish the two.

EMAIL FIELD

The next type of input is for email addresses.

```
<input type="email" />
```

It looks, again, just like a regular text field but most browsers will check to see if the content typed inside the control matches that of an email address. If it doesn't, it will display some sort of warning effect.

Good format: siteraw@siteraw.com

Bad format: siteraw

An email field

These warning effect vary from browser to browser.

In this case, as you can see in the above illustration, the field containing content that doesn't match the pattern of an email address has been automatically highlighted in red. Mobile browsers will also display a specific keyboard for these types of entry fields, usually one containing mail-related special characters (such as @).

URL FIELD

URL fields are very similar, they indicate that the visitor is supposed to enter a URL (website address).

```
<input type="url" />
```

As with the email field, some browsers will check to see if the content entered matches the pattern of a web address, and if not display an appropriate warning effect.

Good format: http://www.siteraw.com

Bad format: siteraw

A URL field

Same principle, mobile browsers will display a keyboard suitable for entering web addresses containing URL-specific special characters (/, .com).

NUMBER FIELD

This form control is used to display a numeric input field.

```
<input type="number" />
```

The field is often displayed with a set of increment and decrement arrows that allow you to change the value you entered. You can also use your up and down keys to get the same effect.

$$(X - 57) / 699 + 2 = 5$$

Answer: 2154|

A number field

You can also set restrictions on what numbers are accepted as well as the increment step with the following attributes.

- min : the minimum allowed value
- max : the maximum allowed value
- step : the legal increment interval, by how does the value increase or decrease when using the arrows (also affects accepted values)

You can play around with these attributes to customize your number fields.

```
<input type="number" min="10" max="50" step="5" />
```

This control will accept any value between 10 and 50 by increment of 5 (i.e. 10, 15, 20, [...], 45, 50). Remember that minimum and maximum values are included.

RANGE FIELD

Range input fields, also called slider controls, are useful when you want the user to enter an approximate value.

```
<input type="range" />
```

Here is what it looks like depending on the browser you're using.

A range field

The default range is 0 to 100 with a step of 1 but those values can be adjusted using the properties we just covered: `min`, `max` and `step`. Try moving the slider to the left or right to change the value of the field.

DATE FIELD

Date fields are used for input controls containing a date. Depending on the browser, you may see a date picker similar to that of Windows' calendar.

```
<input type="date" />
```

Here is what it looks like.

A date field

This type of field demands a full date (day, month and year).

There also exist alternatives to date which only require some of those parameters: month, time, week, datetime.

Try them out.

PHONE FIELD

Finally, the phone field is used for entering a phone number.

```
<input type="tel" />
```

It doesn't amount to much visually, but on most mobile browsers the keyboard will automatically shift to numerical keys which make entering a number that much easier.

A phone field (mobile keyboard)

That's all for input fields, now let's cover other types of form controls.

There are two other types of input fields, hidden and file. The hidden field is, as its name implies, not visually rendered on the web page although it can be seen in the source code. It's useful for passing on data to the target page without the user having to interact with the specific form control or be otherwise involved in the transmission process. The file control simply provides a way for the user to upload a file from his computer. We won't be using any of these in this chapter, but it's always useful to know them (particularly the former).

OPTION CONTROLS

HTML input fields are pretty cool by themselves, and with CSS the possibilities for customization are nearly endless. Below is just one example of what we can achieve.

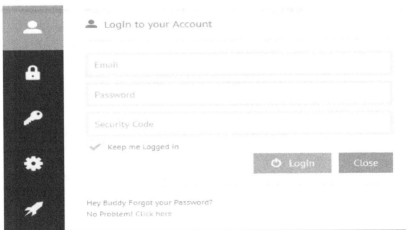

A basic form with CSS

But HTML offers much more than input fields for building your forms. Option controls allow the user to select one or more values from a list of possibilities. There are three methods to provide a list of option in your HTML forms.

- checkboxes
- radio buttons
- drop-down menus

Let's see what they do and how they differ.

CHECKBOXES

Checkbox provide the user with a list of possible entries from which he can choose one or more values. To create checkboxes in HTML we'll be once again using the <input /> element, this time specifying the checkbox type. Don't forget to give it a name and, in case you want to attach a label to it, an id attribute.

```
<input type="checkbox" name="siteraw"
id="siteraw" />
```

Each checkbox is considered an individual element in HTML, so there is no "checkbox container" like you might expect.

As such, creating a checkbox list is just a matter of adding one checkbox element after the other.

```html
<form method="post" action="target.html">
    <p>SiteRaw is...</p>

    <p>

        <input type="checkbox" name="amazing"
id="amazing" /> <label for="amazing">Amazing!</
label><br />

        <input type="checkbox"
name="ineffable" id="ineffable" /> <label
for="ineffable">Ineffable!</label><br />

        <input type="checkbox" name="awesome"
id="awesome" checked /> <label
for="awesome">Awesome!</label><br />

        <input type="checkbox" name="overrated"
id="overrated" disabled /> <label
for="overrated">Presumptuously overrated!</
label>

    </p>
</form>
```

And here is the result.

SiteRaw is...

☐ Amazing!
☐ Ineffable!
☑ Awesome!
☐ Presumptuously overrated!

HTML checkboxes

Perhaps you noticed two new attributes in our HTML code: checked and disabled.

You may also have guessed their function: to have a box be checked by default and to prevent one from being checked respectively. We don't want people having the wrong opinions after all.

 While all attributes are in theory required to have a value, this exception is permitted since HTML5. If you don't like this syntax you can always write the slightly more redundant checked="checked" *and* disabled="disabled", *they both produce the same result. This practice is called attribute minimization and only works in certain cases when the value of the attribute is identical to its name.*

Since we linked the labels to their respective checkboxes, clicking on a label will automatically check or uncheck the appropriate box. Try it.

 How do I limit the selection to only one checkbox? At the moment, I can choose more than one option!

That's the purpose of checkboxes: to allow multiple choices.

If you want to limit the selection to only one value, you should try using radio buttons.

That's what we'll be covering next.

Radio buttons

Radio buttons are another type of option control, which allow the user to select one - and only one - value from a list of possibilities. To create a radio button, we'll use once again the <input /> element with the radio type.

The main difference between radio buttons and checkboxes is that while the latter were all considered distinct HTML elements, the former need to be grouped together in order to work as intended. In practice, that means that all radio buttons of a same group will share an identical name attribute.

 So how do we distinguish one option from another then?

Easy. We simply add a value to each button.

```
<form method="post" action="target.html">
    <p>SiteRaw is...</p>

    <p>

<input type="radio" name="siteraw"
id="amazing" value="amazing" /> <label
for="amazing">Amazing!</label><br />

    <input type="radio" name="siteraw"
id="ineffable" value="ineffable" /> <label
for="ineffable">Ineffable!</label><br />

    <input type="radio" name="siteraw"
```

```
id="awesome" value="awesome" checked /> <label
for="awesome">Awesome!</label><br />

        <input type="radio" name="siteraw"
id="overrated" value="overrated" disabled
/> <label for="overrated">Presumptuously
overrated!</label>

    </p>
</form>
```

This should produce the following result.

SiteRaw is...

○ Amazing!
○ Ineffable!
◉ Awesome!
○ Presumptuously overrated!

HTML radio buttons

As you can tell, the checked and disabled attributes also work for radio buttons.

 Why do we use the same name on each option? I don't get it.

This is necessary when you want to have multiple radio buttons belonging to the same group.

If they weren't linking together via their name attribute, the browser would have no way of knowing which group each button belongs to and thus the user would be able to select more than one option... which defeats the purpose of this form control, since we already have checkboxes for that.

1. Do you have pets?

   ◉ Yes

   ○ No

2. Which pets do you have?

   ☐ Dog

   ☑ Cat

   ☑ Lizard

   ☐ Bird

Checkboxes and radio buttons

If you have more than one option field, you will want to give a unique name to each group in order to distinguish between them.

The best way to summarize: one name, one option group, different values within that group.

Remember that while more than one form control can have the same name, as we know id *attributes must be unique and therefore cannot be shared by multiple HTML elements. The workaround is to match the* id *with the* value *of each control, as I did in my demonstration code.*

DROP-DOWN MENUS

Drop-down menus, also called select boxes or simply dropdowns, are another way of offering a selection amongst several possibilities.

Just like radio buttons, drop-down lists only permit one selection per menu. Here is an example of what it can look like.

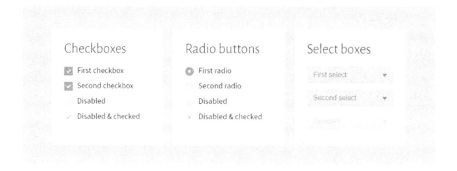

HTML form elements

In this case, we'll need both a container element to specify the beginning and end of the list, and an option element for each item contained within the menu.

The container element is <select> and the item element is <option>. In addition, we'll give the <select> element a name and each <option> item a distinct value.

See the code on the next page.

```
<form method="post" action="target.html">
    <p><label for="siteraw">SiteRaw is...</
label></p>

    <p>
        <select name="siteraw" id="siteraw">
            <option value="amazing">Amazing</
option>
            <option
value="ineffable">Ineffable</option>
            <option value="awesome"
selected>Awesome</option>
            <option value="overrated"
disabled>Overrated</option>
        </select>
    </p>
</form>
```

And the result.

HTML drop-down menu

The `disabled` attribute still works fine, but if you want an option to be selected by default it's no longer checked but `selected`.

OPTION GROUPS

You can also group several options with the <optgroup> element. Give it a `label` attribute to create a title for each group.

```
<select name="siteraw" id="siteraw">
    <optgroup label="Positive">
        <option value="amazing">Amazing</option>
        <option value="ineffable">Ineffable</option>
        <option value="awesome">Awesome</option>
    </optgroup>

    <optgroup label="Neutral" disabled>
        <option value="okay">Okay</option>
        <option value="overrated">Overrated</option>
    </optgroup>
</select>
```

You can see the result below.

Drop-down menu with option groups

Groups themselves can't be selected, they are just used to semantically categorize the items contained within the drop-down list. You may have noticed that this time I applied the disabled attribute to the <optgroup> element rather than an individual <option> tag. This has the effect of disabling the entire group and every item contained within.

 Don't confuse the label attribute, employed exclusively with drop-down menus, and the <label> element which is used for adding a caption to a form control.

You can of course use CSS to customize your drop-down menus. Here is an example of the type of effect you can achieve.

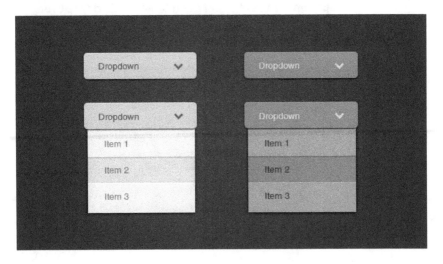

Drop-down menus with CSS

Don't forget that you can apply different properties to each specific element, from the container to each individual item.

SENDING THE FORM

We've covered nearly every component of HTML forms, all that's left is to add push button to confirm our data and finally send it. But first, there are a few more useful features that we should introduce.

FIELD GROUPS

Just as we can separate the items of our drop-down menus into distinct groups, so can we divide the controls of our forms into distinct fields with the <fieldset> element. You can also add a caption for each field using the <legend> tag.

Here is an example.

```
<form method="post" action="target.html">

    <fieldset>
        <legend>About you</legend>

        <p><label for="name">What's your
name?</label> <br/> <input type="text"
name="name" id="name" /></p>

        <!-- Stuff -->
    </fieldset>

    <fieldset>
        <legend>About SiteRaw</legend>

        <p>Is SiteRaw awesome?</p>
```

```
        <p>
                <input type="radio" name="siteraw"
value="yes" id="yes" checked /> <label
for="yes">Yes</label><br />

                <input type="radio" name="siteraw"
value="no" id="no" disabled /> <label
for="no">No</label>
        </p>

        <!-- More stuff -->
    </fieldset>

</form>
```

The result obtained is shown in the figure below.

HTML fieldset element

You can customize your field groups with CSS to make them stand out more, or less. It's up to you.

FORM SPECIFIC ATTRIBUTES

There exist additional attributes that are employed almost exclusively with form controls and that allow you to alter either the way the form is presented, how it is processed or even the user interactions with individual elements. We've already seen a few of them and there are still some others that we've yet to discover.

DEFAULT SELECTION

Nothing new here, to automatically select an option we only need `checked` for checkboxes and radio buttons or `selected` for drop-down menu items.

```
<input type="radio" name="siteraw"
value="siteraw" checked />
```

DISABLING A FIELD

Disabling a field is, as we saw, only a matter of adding the `disabled` attribute to the appropriate control.

```
<input type="text" name="siteraw" disabled />
```

AUTOMATIC FOCUS

You can automatically place the focus on one element of your form with the `autofocus` attribute. When the visitor loads the page, the affected element will automatically be focused on.

```
<input type="text" name="siteraw" autofocus />
```

Obviously, there can only be one such element per page.

MANDATORY FIELDS

You can also make a field mandatory by assigning it the `required` attribute.

```
<input type="text" name="siteraw" required />
```

Most modern browsers will prevent the form from being submitted if all mandatory fields aren't filled out. In addition, a visual notification will often be provided to inform the user that a completing specific field is required. The default visual effects themselves will vary depending on the browser but you can always use the CSS `:required` and `:invalid` pseudo-formats to apply your own.

FORM BUTTONS

Finally, the missing piece of the form puzzle: buttons. Clickable buttons are a useful addition to your forms and all but necessary to provide a way for the user to confirm and submit the information. Once again we will be using the <input /> element. We'll be changing the value of the type attribute depending on what sort of button we want. Here are the values it can take.

- submit : sends the form data to the page specified in the form's action attribute.
- reset : resets the value of every field contained in the form.
- button : a generic button which will have no effect, by default. It's useful when using Javascript to perform dynamic actions on the page.

To change the text contained within the button itself, use the value attribute.

```
<input type="submit" value="Submit" />
```

The result is shown below.

HTML submit button

Of course, having a single submit button isn't very useful. Let's try attaching it to a fictitious login form where the user first has to enter his username and password before submitting the form and, if the information is correct, accessing a member-only area. Here is the demonstration HTML code.

```html
<form method="post">
    <p>
        <input type="text" name="username"
placeholder="username" required />
    </p>
    <p>
        <input type="password" name="password"
placeholder="password" required />
    </p>
    <p>
        <input type="submit" name="login"
value="Login" />
    </p>
    <p>Not registered? <a href="signup.
html">Create an account</a></p>
</form>
```

You can see the result below.

HTML only login form

And since we haven't done much CSS in this chapter, now is the opportunity to stylize our page a little. The exact same code, this time with CSS.

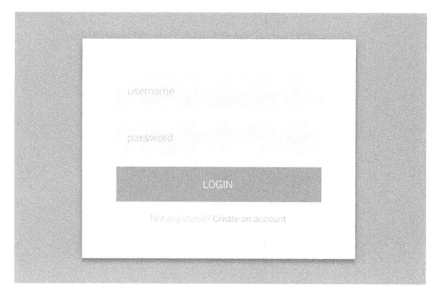

A login form with CSS

When the user clicks the "Login" button, the data will be submitted to the target page (here it's the same page as the form, since we didn't provide an action attribute).

The problem is that you we can't do much more with HTML and CSS only, we will need a server-side programming language (such as PHP or ASP.NET) to interpret, process and manipulate said data. There are free courses on both these languages available for free on SiteRaw, just like this one, but for now let's finish our HTML and CSS tutorial before worrying about adding another language to the mix.

AUDIO AND VIDEO

In the same way that we can embed images in our web pages with the <img /> tag, we can (almost) just as easily insert audio and video web players elements with <audio> and <video>. This is an HTML novelty, since before the current version - HTML 5 - you had to involve a plugin such as Flash or Silverlight, solutions which come with their own sets of inconveniences. In this chapter we we'll learn how to create our own audio and video players, this means we will be able to play our own audio and video content on our web pages with these new HTML 5 elements... just like most video streaming sites. Why did I wait until now to introduce these elements?

Audio and video sharing aren't often used because of the size of multimedia files. Each time a user wants to watch your video or listen to your audio content, they will have to load a file that is often much heavier, thus requiring more bandwidth, than the web page itself.

Which is why webmasters often prefer third-party solutions, such as the aforementioned video streaming sites, to handle their multimedia content. Nevertheless, you might want to embed your own audio tracks or videos somewhere in your website at some point or another, so it's always best to know how these elements work and how to use them yourself. And thanks to HTML 5, this is incredibly easy to do.

AUDIO AND VIDEO FORMATS

Before diving into the implementation of our audio and video players, we should talk about audio and video formats. If you remember, when we talked about images in one of the first chapters of this tutorial, we spent a little while presenting the three main image formats.

The same dilemma exists for audio and video content: what are the different formats and which one should I use? And if learning about a bunch of new formats wasn't enough, there is an added difficulty when dealing with audio and video data: not all formats are supported by all browsers.

Better get started.

AUDIO FORMATS

There are many formats used for storing digital audio data, and most of those used with HTML5 are naturally compressed to reduce the file size.

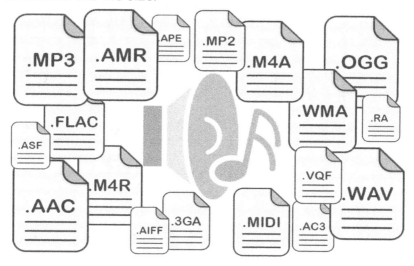

Audio file formats

We will cover the four formats used most often on websites.

- MP3: one of the most widely used formats, compatible with pretty much every modern browser.
- AAC: mainly used by Apple via iTunes, also compatible with all modern browsers.
- OGG: a free format, not protected by patent, but also incompatible with IE, Edge and Safari.
- WAV: compatible with all excepted IE, this is an uncompressed format and should therefore be avoided.

You can't really go wrong with MP3, as only older versions of Firefox don't support it.

But you can provide a OGG alternative as we'll see later on in this tutorial. Here is a compatibility chart.

Format	IE	Edge	Firefox	Chrome	Safari
MP3	Yes	Yes	Yes	Yes	Yes
AAC	Yes	Yes	Yes	Yes	Yes
OGG	-	-	Yes	Yes	-
WAV	-	Yes	Yes	Yes	Yes

Avoid OGG alone due to compatibility and WAV because it's an uncompressed (larger) file format. Compatibility between browsers and audio formats may change in the future, so if you're reading this tutorial a year after publication keep in mind that things may have evolved a little. There are of course other audio formats, but they are very seldom used on HTML web pages.

Video formats

Just as with audio, there are different kinds of video formats, often recognizable by their file extension. We will cover the three most used ones: MP4, WebM and OGG. You may also have heard of the AVI format, it isn't used in HTML5 as it is unsupported by most browsers.

On the next page is a compatibility chart for video formats.

Format	IE	Edge	Firefox	Chrome	Safari
MP4	Yes	Yes	Yes	Yes	Yes
WebM	-	Yes	Yes	Yes	-
OGG	-	-	Yes	Yes	-

The best option is to go with MP4 as it works on all modern browsers.

 To get unnecessarily technical, it isn't so much the format (file container) as the codec (compression standard) that determines compatibility. The video codec for MP4 is usually H.264, which is understood by all modern browsers, so it really doesn't affect our use of video elements in HTML.

AN AUDIO ELEMENT

Now that we've covered the theory of audio and video files, let's move on to the practice.

To insert an audio element in our web page we will be using the <audio> tag. We must also specify the location of the audio content with the src attribute, just like with images.

Here is a code example of a basic audio player in HTML.

```
<audio src="siteraw.mp3"></audio>
```

It's pretty cool up until you load your page and notice a very minor issue: nothing shows up. It's also very normal, as this code only asks the browser to fetch the metadata (information about the file such as its length, etc) and do nothing else. To display an actual audio player we must add the `controls` attribute. It doesn't require a value.

```
<audio src="siteraw.mp3" controls></audio>
```

The visual appearance of the audio player will vary from browser to browser. You can change the design of the audio element, add or remove buttons and stylize the player, but it requires a scripting language such as Javascript in addition to CSS so we won't cover it here. We can, however, customize our audio player by adding the following attributes.

- `controls` : adds play and pause buttons, a volume control and everything else you would expect on a multimedia player.
- `autoplay` : automatically starts playing once the element is loaded (not recommended as it's very annoying).
- `loop` : the audio file will be played in a loop, once you reach the end it will start back at the beginning.
- `muted` : the audio output starts muted.

- `preload` : determines whether the audio content can be preloaded. It can take the following values: `auto` to load the entire file, `metadata` to load only the metadata and `none` to preload nothing and save a little more bandwidth. You can't force the browser to preload your content, it's always the browser that decides whether to do so or not (for example, most mobile browser will never preload anything).

You can try these out to see how they work in greater details.

 Why do we open the <audio> tag only to close it immediately afterwards? Wouldn't it have made more sense if it was a standalone tag?

That's because unlike with <img />, a standalone tag, you can add content inside the <audio> element. Said content will only be displayed if the browser doesn't support the <audio> feature, allowing you to display an error message and/or provide a fallback solution.

```
<audio src="siteraw.mp3" controls>

  <p>Your browser sucks! Stop using noob
browsers!</p>

  <p>You can still <a href="siteraw.
mp3">download the audio file</a>.</p>

</audio>
```

MULTIPLE AUDIO FORMATS

It's possible that some browsers support the <audio> element but not the MP3 format (it happens with some older versions of Firefox). In this case, rather than a cumbersome fallback solution we can simply provide an alternative file with a different format. To do so we won't apply a src attribute to the audio player itself, instead we will add one or more <source> elements inside the <audio> tag.

```
<audio controls>
    <source src="siteraw.mp3"></source>
    <source src="siteraw.ogg"></source>
</audio>
```

The browser will automatically interpret whichever format it recognizes. Note that you can also add an error notice or fallback with this setup, you just have to add your content after the <source> tags.

A VIDEO ELEMENT

Just like we did with <audio>, we can add a video player to our web page using the <video> element. We'll need the src attribute to specify the location of our video file.

```
<video src="siteraw.mp4"></video>
```

Once again, you'll be disappointed if you leave your code like that: right now it only fetches the video metadata. Let's add a `controls` attribute to display our video player.

```
<video src="siteraw.mp4" controls></video>
```

There are other attributes you can play with, most of which are similar to those of the audio element.

- `controls` : adds play and pause buttons, a volume control, full-screen mode and so on.
- `autoplay` : the video starts playing automatically once it's done loading.
- `loop` : the video will be played in a loop, starting over each time it's finished.
- `muted` : the audio output of the video starts muted.
- `preload` : works just like with audio, same values. If nothing is specified the browser will just use the first frame of the video.
- `poster` : the location of the "thumbnail" image to be shown until the video is played.

As with the audio player, you can provide content inside the <video> tag that will only be displayed if the element is unsupported and the browser doesn't recognize the tag.

MULTIPLE VIDEO FORMATS

And just like with our audio player, we can provide several file with different formats to allow the browser to pick whichever one it can read. The methodology is exactly the same, we just use the <source> tag instead of the src attribute.

```
<video poster="siteraw.png" controls>

    <source src="siteraw.mp4"></source>

    <source src="siteraw.ogg"></source>

</video>
```

It's a common practice to indicate the primary file first and add the alternatives after, as we did in our example.

TEXT TRANSCRIPT

There is one last feature we need to cover: text transcripts. You can provide subtitles or any other type of timed text overlays to enhance your videos. It's a little more intricate than what we've seen up until now as you'll need to create a file containing your desired text with a specific format. But first, let's introduce a new HTML element: <track>. It's a child element of <video>, meaning it goes inside, and it needs a src attribute that points towards the location of the text transcript file.

This file should be in WebVTT format (extension .vtt). We don't have one for the moment so just enter anything you want. Here is my HTML code.

```
<video src="siteraw.mp4" controls>

    <track kind="subtitles" src="siteraw.
vtt"></track>

</video>
```

I also gave it a kind attribute which indicates the type of text to be displayed. This attribute is only useful for semantic purposes and can take the following values: captions, chapters, descriptions, metadata or subtitles.

You aren't limited to only one <track>. For instance, if you have several language options for your subtitles you can add several <track> elements one after the other. In this case, use the default attribute (it doesn't require a value) on one of them to make it the default element.

```
<video src="siteraw.mp4" controls>

    <track kind="subtitles" src="siteraw_
en.vtt" default></track>

    <track kind="subtitles" src="siteraw_
de.vtt"></track>

</video>
```

It doesn't work! There are no subtitles on my videos.

That's because you don't have a WebVTT file. Let's create one.

HTML FOR CONTENT, CSS FOR STYLE

The first step is obviously to create a WebVTT file, in my case I'll name it `siteraw.vtt`. A WebVTT (Video Text Tracks) file contains cues, written in a specific format, that communicate to the browser what text to display as well as how and when to display it. Here is the format of a generic WebVTT file.

```
WEBVTT

{START} --> {END}
{TEXT}
```

Every file must start with the WEBVTT string. After that, it's just a matter of providing the start and end times of your text on one line, immediately followed on the next line by the text itself. You can repeat this two-line process for each individual subtitle or other type of text.

```
WEBVTT

00:00:01.000 --> 00:00:05.000
Why is SiteRaw so awesome?

00:00:06.000 --> 00:00:15.000
Because <i>SiteRaw</i> is the most awesome website!
```

402

In the above code, we defined the first subtitle as *"Why is SiteRaw so awesome?"* and set it to appear on the video for four seconds, between the first and fifth second. Same with the second subtitle which will appear between the sixth and fifteenth second. As you can see from the last line, you can include formatting tags in your subtitles: <b>, <i> and <u> for bold, italic and underline respectively. Here is what the result looks like.

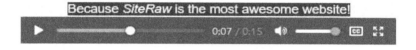

HTML video player with subtitles

You can also customize the subtitles with CSS with the ::cue pseudo-element. Note that not all CSS properties are applicable here, so limit yourself to those relevant to text and background stylization.

```
video::cue {
    background: greenyellow;
    color: black;
}
```

Try it out.

RESPONSIVE DESIGN WITH MEDIA QUERIES

A common annoyance amongst webmasters concerns the handling of the visitor's screen resolution, an issue that only got compounded with the advent of smartphones, tablets and other non-PC electronic devices that can browse the Internet and which all possess different screen sizes.

Let's imagine you just finished building your website and even took the time to embellish it with (what you claim is) the web's most jaw-dropping design. But this design, as elegant as it may be, will usually have a specific width. Say around 900 pixels. By contrast, my iPhone screen is 5.5 inches wide: 330 pixels. What would happen should I try accessing your site with my phone is that I would only be able to display the top-left corner and would have to use the very irritating browser scrollbars just to be able to see the totality of your page.

Imagine having to scroll left to right ad nauseam for each line or each sentence. Even if you were to use a relative width for your design, which is defined in percentage rather than pixels or inches, you could still mess up your layout by having an image, a video player or any other HTML element of which the width is superior to that of a smartphone screen. So what is the solution?

A *responsive design* using CSS media queries.

INTRODUCTION TO MEDIA QUERIES

You can think of media queries as conditions for the application of a CSS code. Very often these conditions will be related to the screen resolution, viewport or output device of the user.

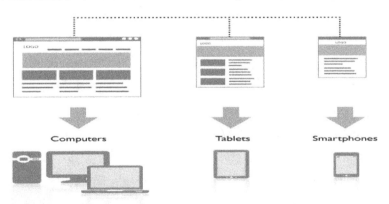

A different layout for each device

Every media query is comprised of two parts: the **conditions** and the **rules**, the latter of which are only applied if the conditions are met.

IMPLEMENTING MEDIA QUERIES

There are two ways to implement media queries: in the HTML file or the CSS file. Let's see how they differ.

WITHIN THE HTML

This method consists of loading one or more additional CSS files if the media query conditions are met. We all know how to link the HTML document with an external style sheet. It's something we learned to do as soon as we discovered CSS.

```
<link rel="stylesheet" href="style.css" />
```

You can add an additional <link /> tag with a media attribute which will contain the conditions required for this new CSS file to be loaded and its properties to be applied to our page.

This is known as making a media query.

```
<link rel="stylesheet" media="screen and (max-width: 1280px)" href="small_resolution.css" />
```

The value of the media attribute is the condition.

We will see what `screen and (max-width: 1280px)` means and how you can create your own media queries in a few moments. Just know that you can provide several CSS files for your web page: one to be applied by default and another one, or more, that are only applied if the media conditions are met. These new CSS files don't nullify the default one, they simply add additional properties and sometimes replace existing rules.

WITHIN THE CSS

My preferred method for using media queries is to place them directly in the same CSS document as the default rules. The main advantage is that we don't need to manage multiple style sheets. To do so, all we need is to write @media followed by the condition.

```
@media screen and (max-width: 1280px)
{
    /* CSS properties go here */

}
```

Any CSS rule you want applied only if the conditions are fulfilled are to be placed inside the braces.

MEDIA FEATURES

Perhaps you may have intuitively grasped what the media query does. Our example `screen and (max-width: 1280px)` is a condition which checks if the user's output device is a conventional computer screen and if the maximum width of said screen is 1,280 pixels.

You can see that there are two conditions to be met: the **type** of output device and its **maximum width**. If we only wanted to check the former, we would only need to write `screen`. There are many of such rules you can use to build your own media queries. Here are a few.

MEDIA TYPES

Media types describe the general category of an output device. Here are the different options.

- `all` : suitable for all devices (default).
- `screen` : conventional computer screen.
- `print` : for printing and print preview.
- `speech` : intended for speech synthesizers.

There used to be many more media types such as `handheld` for mobile browsers and `tv` for TV screens but they were depreciated.

MEDIA FEATURES

Media feature expressions are very similar but usually require a value and are written between parentheses to differentiate them from media types. Their purpose is to test for specific characteristics of the user agent, output device or environment. Here are a few of the most useful.

- `width` : the width of the viewport (ex. `1280px`).
- `height` : the height of the viewport (ex. `720px`).
- `orientation` : device orientation (`landscape` or `portrait`).
- `aspect-ratio` : width-to-height aspect ratio (ex. `9/5`).
- `color` : color management in bits-to-pixels (ex. `8`).
- `pointer` : how accurate is the primary input device (`none`, `coarse` or `fine`).
- `scripting` : is scripting (e.g. Javascript) available (`none`, `initial-only`, `enabled`).

There are many more media features but these are the essential ones.

 You can prefix the majority of these expressions with either `min-` or `max-`. This is particularly useful when dealing with dimensions.

LOGICAL OPERATORS

You may want to create a media query that depends on multiple conditions, such as in our first example.

For that purpose we can use these three logical operators: and, not and , (comma, for "or"). Here is how they work.

CONJUNCTION OPERATOR

The and operator is used to combine multiple conditions together into a single media query. All conditions must be met for the CSS to be applied (conjunction).

```
@media all and (min-width: 800px) and (max-
width: 1280px)
```

The above code targets all output devices between 800 pixels and 1280 pixels wide.

NEGATION OPERATOR

The not keyword inverts the meaning of an entire media query (negation). It will negate the entire media query it is applied to not just the specific media type of the condition.

```
@media not screen and (scripting: none)
```

To fulfill the conditions in the above code, the user must not be on a computer screen and not have scripting disabled.

DISJUNCTION OPERATOR

Each query in a comma-separated (,) list is treated separately from the others. If any of the conditions in such a list is met, the entire media statement returns true.

```
@media (min-height: 680px), screen and
(orientation: portrait)
```

The above query will return true if either the minimum height is 680 pixels, or if the user is on a screen with a portrait orientation.

There is also a fourth logical operator called only. *Some older browsers that don't know media queries can still interpret the beginning of the rule: they can read* @media screen *but not the rest of the rule, thus applying the style to all screens even if the rest of the conditions aren't met. Writing* @media only screen *prevents that.*

PRACTICAL APPLICATIONS

Now that we've covered the theory of media queries it's time to put what we know into practical application. We're going to need a baseline HTML document to work with, it can be anything you want as long as it has at least a title and a paragraph to test our queries.

Since I'm lazy, mine will have only a title and a paragraph.

```
<h1>Welcome to SiteRaw</h1>

<p>SiteRaw is the most awesome site on the
web.</p>
```

Now let's add our default CSS.

```
h1 { color: red; }

p { font-style: italic; }
```

And finally our media query with conditional CSS rules. You can add it immediately following your default CSS code.

```
h1 { color: red; }

p { font-style: italic; }

@media (max-width: 680px) {

    h1 { color: green; }

    p { color: blue; }

}
```

Try loading the page in your browser and then changing the dimensions of your window. As long as the width of your window is at least 680 pixels, only the default CSS will be applied (red titles and italic paragraphs).

But as soon as the width goes under the 680 pixels floor, the additional style contained within the media query command is added (green titles and blue paragraphs). This is the principle behind responsive design: dynamically changing the website layout depending on the visitor's resolution.

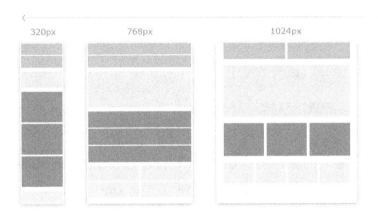

Media queries in CSS

Our code was just a demonstration, as you won't be using media queries to change the color of your text... it's mostly used for adjusting dimensions, removing (via `display: none;`) some blocks that are just too large for handheld devices and rearranging the design of your pages to be readable on small screens and other web supports.

A RESPONSIVE WEBSITE

Now that we know how media queries work and how to apply them using CSS, let's move on to building an actual responsive design. Our goal is to have a website layout that is compatible with both computer screens as well as handheld devices such as mobile phones and tablets. Since we already have a fully functional website from our building your website chapter, we'll being using the same HTML and CSS code.

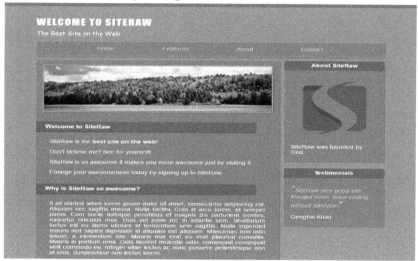

Our HTML and CSS website

While this website layout works (very) well on computers, things start to go a little south when the screen size is less generous. Try reducing the width of your browser window to mimic the approximate dimensions of tablets and mobile phones. The first step in creating responsive designs is to identify what needs to be dynamically modified via media queries.

Since our layout is organized in blocks, it's just a matter of assessing which ones are raising issues when the dimensions of the browser are reduced.

- <body> : 760 pixels wide, let's change that to a maximum width
- <header> : no problems here since there are no fixed dimensions
- <nav> : takes up too much space, let's remove it
- <article> : same as with the <body>
- <aside> : takes too much space, let's put it under <article>
- <footer> : no problems

The beauty of responsive designs with media queries is that you don't need to touch a single line of HTML code. We don't even have to edit our default CSS, we can simply add a media query at the end of our stylesheet to apply specific rules if the user's screen is too narrow.

```css
@media (max-width: 760px) {

    body, article { max-width: 760px; width:
100%; padding: 0; }

    section { display: block; }

    nav { display: none; }

    header { text-align: center; }

    article { flex: 0; }

    article h1, article h2 { margin: 25px 0; }

    article p { padding: 0 15px; }
}
```

You can see the result below.

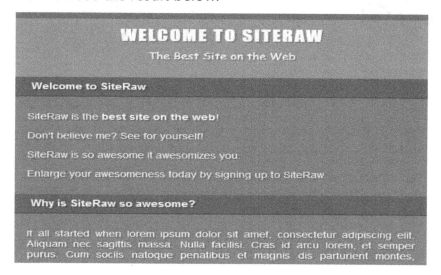

A responsive design

This is the exact same HTML (and CSS) code, we only added one media query that is activated when the browser window is less than 760 pixels wide.

TARGETING MOBILE BROWSERS

Smartphone screens are much narrower than that of their regular computer counterparts. To adapt to this reality, mobile browsers have a built in function that zooms out on the entire page and thus reduces the size of every displayed element. This is called the **viewport**, you can think of it as the initial zoom scale.

And what does that have to do with media queries and responsive designs?

A lot. Just like adolescent boys and people on the Internet, mobile browsers will lie about their size. If you were to try and target mobile phones with the `max-width` condition, it would compare the specified maximum value with that of the viewport of the browser.

The problem is that there is a discrepancy between the viewport width and the actual physical width of the phone. For example, an iPhone using Safari will claim that its width is 980 pixels... that's a little more than 10 inches or 25 centimeters. I doubt that even Steve Jobs' worst prototype ever had a 10 inch wide screen. More than that, it complicates the use of media queries since we can't use `max-width` to accurately target mobile browsers. To resolve that issue, we can either target the device's width itself or adjust the browser's viewport.

DEVICE DIMENSIONS

To target the device's dimensions rather than those of the window, which are affected by the viewport, we can use the media features `device-width` and `device-height` instead of `width` and `height`. You can of course prefix them with either `min-` or `max-` to target the minimum or maximum.

```
@media (max-device-width: 500px)
```

Since mobile devices rarely measure more than 500 pixels wide, we can apply a smartphone specific style to our website using the above media query.

CHANGING THE VIEWPORT

This is a much less common solution, but you can also change the viewport of the browser with a <meta /> HTML element (which goes inside the document header <head>).

```
<meta name="viewport" content="width=500" />
```

To remove the mobile browser zoom that reduces the size of every element on our page, all we need is to match the viewport width with that of the device. The code is nearly identical.

```
<meta name="viewport" content="width=device-width" />
```

These are the two methods for handling the mobile-specific issues of viewport with media queries.

The first method, targeting the device dimensions rather than those of the viewport, is usually the preferred solution.

PART V

CONCLUSION

WEB HOSTING AND DOMAIN NAME

Your website is pretty much complete by now. It's functional, ergonomic, good looking and almost awesome - there is only one awesome website, I won't say it's the one you're looking at right now. The only problem is that since it's stored on your hard drive, you're the only one that can access it. What a shame. Luckily, we'll be learning out to send our website online and thus make it accessible to the entire world in this chapter.

Here is what we'll be covering.

- What is a domain name and how to register one?
- How does web hosting work?
- How to access the cPanel and what does it do?
- How to upload files on the net with a FTP client?

This may seem like a lot to cover, but rest assured that it's all surprisingly easy once you understand the principles behind uploading your site to the web.

A DOMAIN NAME

So what is a domain name? A domain name is simply the address of your website on the web.

For example, `siteraw.com` is a domain name. It's composed of two parts: `siteraw` and `.com`.

- `siteraw` : the domain name itself, which can be chosen freely so long as it's not already registered. It's composed of alphanumerical characters.
- `.com` : the extension, or TLD for top-level domain. There are many TLDs you can choose from including `.com` (the most common), `.net`, `.org`, `.biz` or even country-specific extensions called ccTLDs, such as `.ca` (Canada) or `.uk` (Pakistan).

Websites are often preceded by www, such as in `www.siteraw.com`. This is not technically part of the domain name. It's called a sub-domain, you can have as many as you want or none at all, and www is just the default that has been adopted as convention.

REGISTERING A DOMAIN NAME

Registering a domain name isn't free... if it was, every domain name would already be registered and you wouldn't have any left to choose from. Simple supply and demand. The good news is that it really isn't expensive at all: *a .com name costs between $8 and $9 per year.* It's that cheap, seriously. There are two ways of registering a domain name.

- Through a specialized registrar: these companies will allow you to register as many domain names as you want. Some well-known registrars include Namecheap and GoDaddy.
- Through your web hosting provider: the majority of web hosting services offer you a FREE domain name when you order any hosting plan, that way you can get both the hosting and the domain name from the same source (in our case Bluehost).

The second method is the one we will be covering in this chapter, as it is by far the simplest and most straightforward. Keep in mind that you don't need to use it if you don't want to. Many webmasters don't like using the same provider for both their domain names and their web hosting, which is fine.

WEB HOSTING PLANS

Let's talk about web hosting providers, also called web hosts.

All websites on the Internet are stored in computers called servers, which are turned on 24/7 and whose sole purpose is to make their sites accessible to anyone possessing an Internet connection anywhere in the world.

A web hosting platform

While it's technically possible to host websites on personal computers - which is somewhat similar to what we've been doing up until now - it really isn't practical, for reasons of bandwidth and availability alone. Instead, most individuals and businesses rely on professional web hosting providers.

HTML FOR CONTENT, CSS FOR STYLE

There are three main types of web hosting that correspond to different needs in terms of network resources.

- **Shared hosting**: this is the most basic form of web hosting, the cheapest and the one I recommend 99% of the time for beginner webmasters. As the name implies, your website will be placed on a server managing several websites at once.
- **VPS hosting**: VPS stands for Virtual Private Hosting. This is for larger websites that require more resources than what a shared hosting can typically offer. While the server is still shared by multiple websites, in this case usually less than ten, you are nonetheless allotted resources that aren't shared with anyone.
- **Dedicated server**: dedicated hosting is the heavyweight solution for websites that really need the upgrade. The server handles your website, or websites, and no other. No sharing either bandwidth, disk space or CPU without anyone else. Obviously, this is the most expensive solution and only becomes practical for very large - and visited- websites such as Wikipedia, Youtube and so on.

If you want a real estate analogy, you can think of shared hosting an apartment, VPS as a condo and dedicated hosting as a house.

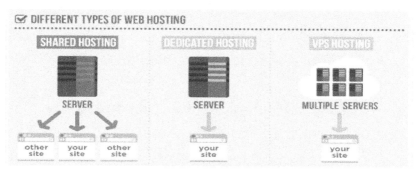

Different types of web hosting

429

In this tutorial we will only cover shared hosting, which for now is the most appropriate solution for your website.

HOSTING YOUR WEBSITE

Just as with domain name registrars, there are many companies that offer web hosting solutions to both individuals and businesses. Amongst the most famous are Hostgator, Bluehost, Hostmonster and GoDaddy. Any of these is a solid choice, but since we have to choose one for this chapter we'll go with Bluehost.

Use this link for the cheapest Bluehost hosting options: GO.SITERAW.COM/BLUEHOST.

Web hosting isn't free, obviously, but Bluehost offers some of the cheapest and most cost-effective solutions to beginner website owners.

For as cheap as $2.95 per month, you get:

- A free domain name
- 50 GB of disk space (more than anyone would ever need)
- UNLIMITED bandwidth (this is important)
- A maximum of 25 sub-domains

There is of course more than one plan you can choose from.

	basic	plus	prime recommended
	normally $7.99	normally $10.99	normally $14.99
	$2.95* per month	$5.45* per month	$5.45* per month
	select	select	select
websites	1	unlimited	unlimited
website space	50 GB	unmetered	unmetered
bandwidth	unmetered	unmetered	unmetered
performance	Standard	Standard	Standard
included domains	1	1	1
parked domains	5	unlimited	unlimited
sub domains	25	unlimited	unlimited

Bluehost hosting plans

For beginner website owners I recommend the "prime" plan, $2.95 per month for unlimited bandwidth, 50 GB disk space and a free domain name.

 What do they mean by "bandwidth"?

Bandwidth is the transmission capacity of a network or telecommunication system, the quantity of data that can be sent to your website visitors.

Example: you have a 1 MB image that is loaded 500 times by your visitors, it amounts to 500 MB worth of bandwidth.

(That's the theory, in practice most browsers will cache the image after the first visit thereby avoiding having to load the same file multiple times).

A lot of web hosts will place limits on the amount of bandwidth available to you, which is yet another reason why Bluehost is a very good choice for most webmasters: *you don't have to worry about bandwidth since it's unlimited.*

ORDERING A WEB HOSTING SOLUTION

Now that we're reading to order our web hosting plan, just click the "Get Started Now" button on Bluehost and then select your plan: "basic", "plus" or "prime". You will be taken to a page asking you to choose a free domain name for your website. Just type in what you want as your domain name, and Bluehost will then check to see if it's available.

If it is, you can move on to the next step. If not, you can't really do that much about it aside from picking another one... maybe claim you're Bill Gates' son and should therefore inherit the microsoft.com domain. Might work. All that's left to do is to enter your contact information such as name, country and email address and proceed to payment via Paypal or credit card. Once the payment is processed you will be redirected to a member area and should receive an email containing all the information you need to set up your website.

Save that information as you will need it later.

ACCESSING THE CPANEL

To make your website accessible to anyone possessing an Internet connection, you first have to send your files - HTML pages, CSS style sheets, images, etc. - to your web hosting service. There are essentially two ways to do this: with the **cPanel** or through **FTP** (File Transfer Protocol).

We'll cover both methods, but let's start with cPanel. Once you login on Bluehost or whatever web hosting solution you chose for your website, you will be redirected to a cPanel (control panel) that will look something like what you see in the figure below.

The main cPanel screen

There are a lot of features so it might look a bit overwhelming, but you don't need to know what everything does for now. If you're curious you can always read the documentation.

Just know that the cPanel is where you control and monitor everything that has to do with your website once it is online: file storage, domain name, disk usage, server configuration, databases, backup, cron jobs, email accounts and other additional modules. But for now our site isn't even online, so we'll only bother with one feature: the **File Manager**.

The File Manager is what will allow you to upload your files to your web hosting server and make your site accessible to the world.

Click on the "File Manager" icon and make sure you are in the `public_html` directory before uploading your files. Once you are, just click the upload button and start sending your files to your web hosting server. They should be available on your website, meaning that you just have to enter your domain name (ex. `www.siteraw.com`) in your browser to see the result.

USING A FTP CLIENT

Using the cPanel File Manager is a very fast and efficient way of getting your files online.

434

But since you have to manually send every file one by one, it can get a bit tedious when you have a large amount of content to upload. The other method we'll introduce requires a **FTP client**. FTP stands for File Transfer Protocol and is the standard network protocol used for transferring computer files between a client and server. The FTP client is just the software you download to facilitate the procedure. It can be done without a client, but then we would need to use the command-line interface, something needlessly intricate for what we're attempting to do.

FileZilla, a free FTP client

The FTP client I recommend is FileZilla, which is free and open-source.

The interface may seem confusing at first but it's really straightforward once you get used to it. There are four main areas to consider.

- top : the connection fields as well as a list of messages the program sends and receives. You don't need to pay that much attention to this area unless you get error messages (in red).
- left : the files and folders on your hard drive.
- right : the files and folders on the remote web server (where we want to send our website).
- bottom : the current operations, usually which files are being sent and the percentage of completion.

The first step will be to connect to the remote server.

Connecting to the server

With the cPanel method we could bypass this step since we were already authenticated, but the FTP client needs to know to which remote server we want to send our files. For that we will need three pieces of data: the host address (usually something like `ftp.yourdomain.com`), the username and the password.

These are your FTP credentials and should have been emailed to you when you ordered your web hosting plan. If they weren't or if you forgot them, you can always access them from the cPanel under `File Management` > `FTP Manager`.

There are two ways to connect to the remote server with FileZilla.

- Quickconnect: all you need is to enter your information in the required fields and click Quickconnect.
- Site Manager: this will give you more control over how the connection is made and allow you to store your login information so that you don't have to go through the whole process next time you want to authenticate to the same server.

For the second method, just navigate to `File > Site Manager` and click the `New Site` button. You should arrive on a window similar to what is shown below.

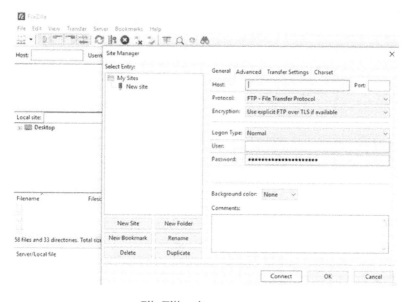

FileZilla site manager

Don't forget to set the authentication type to `Normal` and click `Connect`.

TRANSFERRING FILES

Once you are connected to the web hosting, the right side of the interface - the one that concerns the remove server - should be activated. You can then double-click, or drag-and-drop, any file you want transfered.

It's much faster than using the cPanel, particularly if you have a large quantity of files to upload. This concludes the chapter on domain names and web hosting.

BUILDING ADVANCED WEBSITES

When you first looked at the summary of this tutorial and saw the list of chapters, you were probably thinking something along the line of "*WTF?? I have to learn all this to create a website?*". And now that we're reaching the end of this course you might be asking "Is that it? Did we see everything there is to learn?". Of course not. While I tried to make this tutorial as wide and exhaustive as possible, sometimes at the risk of covering certain fringe subjects of web development that you aren't likely to run into very often such as audio and video elements, there is always something more to learn.

For starters, we only ever covered two languages: HTML and CSS. There are many more aspects to web development that we haven't introduced: client-side scripting languages such as Javascript, server-side programming languages such as PHP, database handling with SQL, web applications with AJAX as well as other technologies related to HTML5 and more.

Don't worry, I won't let you leave this page without inflicting upon you yet another chapter full of bewildering concepts and barbaric terminology.

WHAT WE KNOW

After a brief introduction to the basic text editors (Notepad, Sublime, Brackets) and different web browsers (IE, Firefox, Edge) involved in web development, we learned how to create basic HTML pages by adding titles, paragraphs, emphasis, links and images.

Part I: The basics of HTML5.

After a brief introduction to the basic text editors (Notepad, Sublime, Brackets) and different web browsers (IE, Firefox, Edge) involved in web development, we learned how to create basic HTML pages by adding titles, paragraphs, emphasis, links and images.

Welcome to SiteRaw

SiteRaw is the best site on the web!

Why is SiteRaw so awesome?

- Because it's awesome
- Because I'm awesome
- Because it's SiteRaw

That's why SiteRaw is **awesome** !

Basic elements with HTML

In this part I deliberately avoided talking about CSS. The downside is that our web pages were pretty ugly for the first few chapters, but it provided the benefit of only having to learn one language at the time.

Part II: Web design with CSS3.

After a while, it was inevitable that we started introducing the second aspect of web development: designing the layout with CSS. The chapters may have seem somewhat heavy due to the amount of CSS properties that you had to learn, but that's just the nature of the CSS language.

A demonstration of CSS properties

From colors to backgrounds, gradients to borders, typographical formatting to alignments... there were a lot of

CSS properties we had to cover and I did my best to lessen the repetitiveness of these chapters, notably by providing cool examples of the practical applications of these properties.

Part III: HTML and CSS together.

The third part of this tutorial was about combining what we learned in the previous two, namely the HTML and CSS languages, and taking things even further than what we'd have otherwise expected.

An advanced HTML and CSS website

After a brief theoretical introductory chapter to HTML5 web page structure, we learned about the CSS box model and different types of layouts before building our first complete HTML and CSS website.

This was the chapter you had all been waiting for.

Part IV: Advanced features.

Finally, we introduced a few of the more advanced - and the term is very relative - features of HTML and CSS such as tables, audio and video elements and media queries.

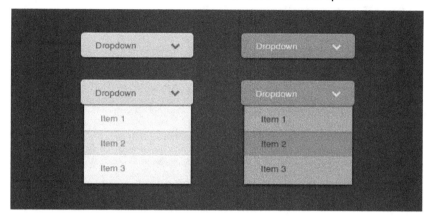

HTML form controls

After seeing how tables work in HTML, we finally got around to seeing forms. While it was pretty cool to learn how to design form layouts by stylizing the different text fields and other controls, it was nonetheless a slightly frustrating chapter as we couldn't actually do anything with our forms once the data was submitted.

We could get the user to send the data contained in the form by clicking a "Submit" button, but we had no way to receive and interpret that data... for that would require a server-side programming language (PHP, ASP.NET).

At the time I promised that we would cover these server-side languages in greater detail, and so we will a little further on in this chapter. But before that let's talk about Javascript.

CLIENT-SIDE LANGUAGES

Is called client-side any computing language that is executed by the client - in most cases, the browser. As such, both HTML and CSS are considered client-side languages since they are interpreted by the user's browser - specifically the layout engine - rather than the server. In addition to HTML and CSS, which are respectively markup and style sheet languages, we can mention a third common website component: **scripting languages such as Javascript**.

The Javascript language

While alternatives to Javascript have existed in the past, we can cite VBScript which was developed by Microsoft, there are currently very little viable substitutes for this language when it comes to client-side scripting. The main reason is that the interpretation of Javascript being handled by the browser's rendering engine, its developers are the ones that have to handle Javascript's implementation... and they probably aren't too eager to repeat the process on yet another language just to provide you with a alternative. What is much more common is to have Javascript libraries such as jQuery or frameworks such as Angular that attempt to simplify some aspects of client-side scripting.

JAVASCRIPT DEMONSTRATION

Since Javascript is interpreted by the browser, you can start using it right away in the same way we've been using HTML and CSS. Here are a few examples of how Javascript works. Just add the following code anywhere on your page.

```
<script type="text/javascript">

    document.write("SiteRaw is awesome!");

</script>
```

This will display the text "SiteRaw is awesome!".

As you may have guessed, <script> is the HTML element used to reference or embed client-side code, usually Javascript.

```
<script type="text/javascript">

    alert("SiteRaw is awesome!");

</script>
```

This will produce an alert window containing the text "SiteRaw is awesome!". The style of the window will depend on which browser you're using.

A Javascript notification window

I won't be going over what each individual Javascript property or function does as this is beyond the scope of this chapter, and there exists a completely free Javascript tutorial right here on SiteRaw (www.siteraw.com) which you can read if you're interested in this language.

THE PURPOSE OF JAVASCRIPT

You're probably wondering why you'd need to learn another language in addition to HTML and CSS.

446

The purpose of scripting languages such as Javascript is to make your pages more interactive.

We can use Javascript to do the following.

- display dialog boxes on the visitor's screen
- provide suggested results (autocomplete) on a search field
- automatically fetch information from another document without reloading the page
- customize the verification of form controls such as verifying if a username is available
- produce draggable, droppable, resizable or otherwise sortable elements
- dynamically change the HTML attributes (usually class) of an element on the click of a button
- implement transitions between the different states of an element

Basically you can edit the HTML and CSS codes of your page dynamically, for example on the click of a button or when the user performs a specific action.

SERVER-SIDE LANGUAGES

The languages we are about to discover here are also programming languages, but they differ from Javascript by the fact that they are interpreted on the server (web host) rather than on the client (browser). Javascript code is executed at the same time as HTML and CSS - technically a little after HTML since the first page to load will be the HTML document - while server-side languages are executed before the page is even loaded. If you want a more visual illustration of the HTTP request/response handshake, take a look at the figure below.

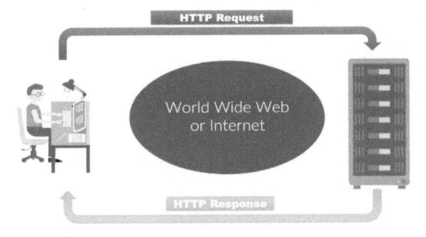

The HTTP protocol

The usual model goes as follows.

- the client sends a request
- the server sends the response
- the page is loaded and rendered in the browser

With the inclusion of a server-side language comes an additional step right after the HTTP request.

- the client sends a request
- the page is generated
- the server sends the response
- the page is loaded and rendered in the browser

What that means is that the visitor will never see any server-side code, as it's executed well before the final output reaches him.

THE DIFFERENT SERVER-SIDE LANGUAGES

Unlike with client-side scripting where you only really have one option with Javascript, there are many server-side languages to choose from.

- **PHP** : one of the simplest and most common server-side languages, PHP is always a good choice for beginners as it is open source, stable and very easy to use. You can read the PHP tutorial on SiteRaw.
- **ASP.NET** : while not technically a language itself but rather an application framework, ASP.NET is perhaps the most efficient and powerful server-side technology for developing large scale web applications. As with PHP, you can read the free ASP.NET tutorial on SiteRaw.
- **JEE (Java)** : somewhat similar to ASP.NET, this Java extension is widely used to build powerful and robust websites.
- **Django (Python)** : an extension of Python that allows quick and easy web development.
- **Ruby on Rails (Ruby)** : an extension of Ruby, the main selling point is the rather impressive number of libraries.

The two most common languages used for web development are PHP and ASP.NET. Which one should you choose? It's really a matter of preference as they both fulfill different needs while simultaneously having a lot of overlapping features, as nearly all programming languages do.

ASP.NET is usually **faster and more efficient**, mainly because it is compiled rather than interpreted (meaning that everything, including HTML, is turned into machine code before being run), but also has a slightly steeper learning curve and is thus more appropriate for large scale applications.

PHP on the other hands is **more accessible to beginners** as nearly every aspect of the language was designed to be as straightforward as possible. It does however suffer from performance issues when compared to ASP.NET, but it's still the recommended choice for novices and small websites. But what can server-side languages do that client-side technologies can't? Let's find out.

ASP.NET is not a language itself, it's a web technology - itself part of the .NET framework - that supports about 25 languages and allows the development of powerful web applications. The most common programming language used with .NET is C#, which you can learn more about via its tutorial on SiteRaw. ASP.NET is "only" the .NET component used for building dynamic web pages.

THE PURPOSE OF SERVER-SIDE LANGUAGES

Server-side languages are what will allow you to create dynamic websites. Here are some examples of website features that require a back-end (server) component.

- member areas
- forums
- newsletters
- visitor counters
- comment systems
- databases
- browser games

Basically anything involving authentication or data management. Server-side languages are what make your site dynamic, in other words it can be constantly updated without it requiring your intervention. The best examples is of course the Internet forum where nearly everything is automated via a server-side language.

Remember the chapter on HTML forms that we couldn't complete because we had no way of processing the data after it was sent?

This also requires a server-side language such as ASP.NET or PHP, and it's actually an incredibly mundane operation that takes at most a few lines of code.

SERVER-SIDE LANGUAGES DEMONSTRATION

It'll be somewhat difficult to show you examples of server-side languages as we did with Javascript since you would need to download a web server (Apache, IIS, nginx, etc.) in order for the code to be properly executed, and this goes well beyond the scope of this chapter. You can however read more about the tools needed to run a server-side language on their respective tutorials right here at SiteRaw.

But just for the sake of satiating your curiosity, here is what PHP code looks like.

```
<body>

    <?php echo "SiteRaw is awesome!"; ?>

</body>
```

This will display the text "SiteRaw is awesome!" between the <body> tags if you have an appropriate web server installed on your computer.

 Server-side code is executed on the server and is thus never shown to the visitor, even if he looks at the source of the page. Users of your website will therefore never see any PHP, ASP. NET or Python code.

WEB APPLICATIONS AND AJAX

There are quite a few newer web technologies that work with HTML5 and were introduced at about the same time.

- **Canvas** : allows you to draw in the web page inside the HTML <canvas> tag. You can draw shapes (triangles, circles, etc.) as well as add text and images, apply graphic filters and more.
- **SVG** : allows you to add vector graphics inside the HTML <svg> tag. Unlike canvases, these graphics can be enlarged as much as you want, which is the principle of Scalable Vector Graphics.
- **Drag & Drop** : allows you to "drag and drop" objects into the web page in the same way that you can drag and drop files onto your desktop. Many e-mail providers such as Outlook use it to allow you to easily add attachments to an email.
- **File API** : provides access to files stored on the visitor's computer with their permission. Often used in combination with Drag & Drop.
- **Geolocalization** : allows you to locate the visitor more or less accurately.
- **Web Storage** : used to store information in the visitor's browser, somewhat similar to cookies.
- **Application Cache** : used for storing certain web pages or other files into cache, useful for creating web applications that can work while offline.
- **Web Sockets** : similar to AJAX, this allows direct communication between the client's browser and the web server without having to reload the page.
- **WebGL** : allows the use of a 3D engine within web pages using the OpenGL 3D standard and directly managed by the user's graphics processing unit (GPU).

Most if not all of these features and technologies require Javascript to operate, which is why they weren't covered in this tutorial.

AJAX APPLICATIONS

AJAX is what allows you to move from simple web development to creating complex web applications that function just like desktop software (except for the fact that they run on a browser). Since client-side languages are used to make your pages more dynamic and functional for the user and server-side languages are used to handle user entries, automation and anything involving persistent data across the pages, what would happen if we were to implement them both in unison?

The best way to describe AJAX (*Asynchronous JavaScript And XML*) is to consider it as a combination of both client-side and server-side, both front-end and back-end working together.

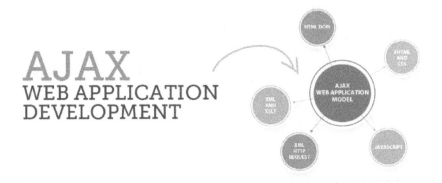

AJAX web application development

You're most likely already familiar with AJAX even if you didn't know the name until you read this chapter.

- Have you ever written an email from a web-based mail provider (Outlook, Gmail, Yahoo)?
- Have you ever had to decipher captchas (characters you type to prove you're human)?
- Have you ever seen a web application with an "autosave" feature (Office Online, Google Docs)?
- Have you ever used a modern comment system (Disqus, Youtube, SiteRaw)?

Then you've been using some form of AJAX without even knowing it... and that's what makes AJAX so practical, it enhances the ergonomics of your website in the most inconspicuous manner. Without AJAX, every time you'd want the client to interact with the server - save a draft, like a video, type in a captcha - the user would have to reload the page entirely in order to submit an HTTP request.

AJAX is the practice of using Javascript to handle these asynchronous requests, meaning that the user will barely even register that an action involving server-side communication is being performed.

THE LIST OF HTML TAGS

The page provides a non-exhaustive list of HTML tags for quick reference purposes. Why isn't it exhaustive? I find that it's better to include less tags in order to focus only on those essential to HTML web development, and also to permit a more accurate classification of these tags into their respective categories. Do you really need to know that <acronym> and <abbr> are used for acronyms and abbreviations? To includes such obscure elements would unnecessarily clog up the page and detract from the essential HTML tag that every webmaster should know on the tip of his fingers.

The list of HTML tags

We've seen all these tags throughout the tutorial so this chapter will naturally only provide a brief description of their usage and specifics. You are free to bookmark or print this page for easy access.

HTML STRUCTURE TAGS

Structure tags deal with the anatomy and metadata of a web page, they don't have any visible properties by default.

Rather, they provide information to the user-agent about the semantic markup of the page. You can read more about these in the HTML structural tags chapter but here is a quick review anyway.

DOCUMENT ELEMENTS

Document level elements are the essential tags you need to define the minimal blueprint of your HTML page.

Tag	Description
<html>	Root element
<head>	Header element
<body>	Body element

This is the minimal code you need to include for any valid HTML page.

```
<!DOCTYPE html>
<html>
    <head>
        <meta charset="utf-8" />
        <title>Title</title>
    </head>

    <body>

    </body>
</html>
```

METADATA ELEMENTS

These tags are located in the header of your page and either provide additional information to the user-agent or indicate the source of another file that needs to be loaded with the page.

Tag	Description
`<title>`	Document title
`<meta>`	Document metadata
`<link>`	External resource
`<script>`	Javascript code
`<style>`	CSS code

STRUCTURAL ELEMENTS

These tags go inside the body of your document and are used to build the skeleton or blueprint of your website layout.

Tag	Description
<header>	Page header
<nav>	Navigation links
<section>	Section element
<article>	Article content
<aside>	Additional information
<footer>	Page footer

TEXT ORGANIZATION

These HTML tags are used to organize your text in a semantically structured way. You can read more about them in the chapter called organize your text at the beginning of this tutorial.

PARAGRAPHS AND LINES

The following tags involve paragraphs, line breaks and other means of content delineation.

Tag	Description
`<p>`	Paragraph
` `	Line break
`<hr />`	Horizontal rule

TITLE ELEMENTS

The tags are used to indicate a section heading, they are ranked by order of importance from highest to lowest.

Tag	Description
`<h1>`	Level 1 title
`<h2>`	Level 2 title
`<h3>`	Level 3 title
`<h4>`	Level 4 title
`<h5>`	Level 5 title
`<h6>`	Level 6 title

EMPHASIS ELEMENTS

The HTML elements are used to add semantic emphasis to portions of your text.

Tag	Description
`<em>`	Emphasis
`<strong>`	Strong importance
`<mark>`	Visual highlight

QUOTATION ELEMENTS

Quotations can easily be managed with these HTML tags.

Tag	Description
`<q>`	Inline quote
`<blockquote>`	Block quote
`<cite>`	Title of a work

EXTERNAL ELEMENTS

Hyperlinks, images, audio elements, video players... anything that involves linking to or embedding an external resource into your page.

Tag	Description
`<a>`	Hypertext link
`<img />`	Image
`<audio>`	Audio player
`<video>`	Video player
`<figure>`	Figure
`<figcaption>`	Figure description

MORE TEXT MARKUP

Some miscellaneous markup tags that can be added inside your paragraphs for semantically marking specific data.

Tag	Description
`<del>`	Deleted text
`<ins>`	Inserted text
`<sup>`	Superscript (exponent)
`<sub>`	Subscript (index)
`<kbd>`	Keyboard entry
`<pre>`	Formatted display
`<progress>`	Progress bar

GENERIC ELEMENTS

These elements have no semantic meaning, they are generally used to target a specific portion of your page via the class or id attributes when applying CSS.

Tag	Description
`<span>`	Inline element
`<block>`	Block element

TABLES AND LISTS

Tables and lists are two of the most common ways to organize data in order to improve readability and accessibility.

Since these elements are constructed with several distinct component, we will need to use several (usually nested) HTML tags to get the desired result.

Tables can seem particularly challenging for beginners due to the quantity of new HTML elements you must know, so I recommend reading the chapter on tables if you forget how these different tags are combined.

TABLE ELEMENTS

Tables are built by combining at least some of the following HTML tags, which you can think of as different necessary components of the table model.

Tag	Description
`<table>`	Table element
`<tr>`	Table row
`<th>`	Header cell
`<td>`	Regular (data) cell
`<caption>`	Table title
`<thead>`	Header section
`<tbody>`	Body section
`<tfoot>`	Footer section

LIST ELEMENTS

There are many types of lists you can use in HTML, the two most common being unordered (bullet) lists and ordered lists.

Tag	Description
<ul>	Bullet list
<ol>	Ordered list
<li>	List item
<dl>	Description list
<dt>	Description term
<dd>	Description details

FORM ELEMENTS

Finally, forms are a very useful way to interact with your visitors by providing them with entry fields to fill out, boxes to check, options to select from a drop-down list and so on.

Here are the essential HTML form element.

Tag	Description
<form>	Form element
<fieldset>	Field group
<legend>	Field group title

`<label>`	Field description
`<input />`	Entry field
`<textarea>`	Multi-line field
`<select>`	Drop-down menu
`<option>`	Drop-down item
`<optgroup>`	Drop-down item group

As I told you at the beginning of this chapter there are several tags that I have deliberately omitted. You will have noticed that in HTML everything is a matter of meaning - we are talking about semantics. What matters most is to use the most appropriate element at all times.

You could in theory do almost anything you want using just the `<div>` and `<span>` generic tags alongside CSS, but your HTML code wouldn't make any sense to non-human user-agents and would thus be penalized. One last time with the golden rule of web development: *HTML for content, CSS for style.*

THE LIST OF CSS PROPERTIES

Just as we did with HTML elements in the previous chapter, we will go over the essential CSS properties used to design website layouts. This list is once again non-exhaustive and classified by property type. Most of the CSS properties we will review have already been covered in greater depths during the course of this tutorial, so if you need more details on how a certain property is declared you can find them in the associated chapters, a direct link is provided when relevant. Let's start by reviewing how CSS code is applied (figure below).

CLASS SELECTOR CSS RULE

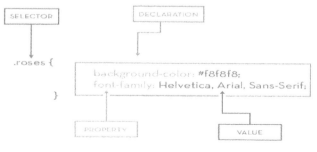

CSS code syntax

The syntax of CSS code declaration is covered in greater detail in the setting up CSS chapter. Remember that you can add as many properties as you want, for each selector, between the curly brackets.

TEXT FORMATTING PROPERTIES

Text formatting is everything that affects the presentation of textual content: bold, italics, underline, font, alignment, letter spacing... Here are the main relevant properties.

Property	Description (Example)
font-family	Font name (Arial)
font-size	Text size (15px)
font-weight	Bold (bold)
font-style	Italic (italic)
text-decoration	Underline, etc. (underline)
text-transform	Uppercase, lowercase... (uppercase)
font-variant	Small caps (small-caps)
@font-face	Custom font
text-align	Horizontal alignment (center)
vertical-align	Vertical alignment (middle)

line-height	Line height (18px)
text-indent	Paragraph indentation (25px)
white-space	Hyphenation (nowrap)
word-break	Word-break (break-all)
text-shadow	Letter shadow (5px 5px 2px blue)

You can read more about these in the text formatting chapter.

COLOR AND BACKGROUND PROPERTIES

The following properties are applied to manage either the color or the background of an element.

Property	Description (Example)
color	Text color (red)
opacity	Transparency (0.5)
background-color	Background color (red)
background-image	Background image (url('img.png'))
background-attachment	Fixed background (scroll)
background-repeat	Background repetition (no-repeat)
background-position	Background position (center)

For more information on these properties you can refer to the color and background chapter of this tutorial.

DIMENSION PROPERTIES

Dimension properties are all the options that involve modifying the height and width of a block-level element. They include the dimensions of the element itself, the padding, the border and the margin.

CSS BOX MODEL

The properties relevant to the CSS box model, minus those involving borders.

Property	Description (Example)
width	Element width (550px)
height	Element height (300px)
min-width	Minimum width (550px)
min-height	Minimum height (300px)
max-width	Maximum width (550px)
max-height	Maximum height (300px)
padding	Inner padding (25px)
margin	Outer margin (25px)

BORDER PROPERTIES

These properties handle border size, shape, color and more.

Property	Description (Example)
border-width	Border width (5px)
border-style	Border type (dotted)
border-color	Border color (red)
border-radius	Rounded borders (5px)
box-shadow	Block shadow (3px 3px 0px red)

You can read more about them in the borders and shadows chapter of this tutorial.

DISPLAY PROPERTIES

Lastly, these properties are used to manipulate the display and positioning of an element or an element group.

Property	Description (Example)
display	Display type (block)
position	Positioning (absolute)
visibility	Visibility (hidden)

overflow	Overflow (hidden)
float	Floating (right)
clear	Clear a float (both)
top	Top offset (20px)
left	Left offset (20px)
right	Right offset (20px)
bottom	Bottom offset (20px)
z-index	Importance if overlap (10)
cursor	Mouse cursor (crosshair)

Done!

Some of you will have noticed that I didn't include every existing CSS property, as I said at the beginning... there are simply too many to list in a single chapter. The goal of this chapter isn't to provide a complete list but rather a quick support when you need to code something in CSS. As such, I only included the most often used CSS properties.

You can bookmark this chapter - and the previous one on HTML elements - for quick access if you ever need to verify how a property is used or what it does.

THE END

This is the end of this book on website creation with HTML and CSS. Seriously, I would like nothing more than to add a "*BONUS: How to broadcast your website into space and mock aliens*" chapter but at this point we've pretty much reached the limits of the HTML and CSS languages.

So what now?

You can of course re-read this book at any time, either in its entirety or just the few select chapters that you feel you haven't fully integrated. You can also bookmark both "memento" chapters - see HTML and CSS - that respectively list the most common tags and properties you will run into when building your website(s).

If still have questions on web development or any other related subject for that matter, feel free to share your mind over at the SiteRaw forums (http://www.siteraw.com).

If you want to go even further down the road of web development, you can also find more tutorials covering additional web technologies - of which the building advanced websites chapter should give you a preview - either online at SiteRaw.com or in eBook or paperback format, just like this book.

Printed in the U.S.A.

ISBN: 1984030205
ISBN-13: 978-1984030207

W W W . S I T E R A W . C O M

www.ingramcontent.com/pod-product-compliance
Lightning Source LLC
LaVergne TN
LVHW022259060326
832902LV00020B/3157